THE NUMISMATIC HISTORY OF EL SALVADOR

BY

JOSE A MEJIA

Copyright © 2011 Jose A Mejia
All rights reserved.
ISBN:10:061548154x
ISBN-13:978-0615481548

To buy the best and rarest Latin American coins visit:
www.alliancelimitedcollectibles.com

Table of Contents

Introduction
Pg 4

Chapter 1: Back in the Days: The Kingdom of Guatemala under Spanish Rule
Pg 6

Chapter 2: A United Front: The Central American Federation
Pg 9

Chapter 3: Independence at Last: The State 1840-1880
Pg 45

Chapter 4: The Beginning of the Liberal State: Land Privatization and the Creation of The Modern State 1880-1892
Pg 67

Chapter 5: La Casa De Moneda: The Central American Mint Limited 1892-1896
Pg 78

Chapter 6: A New Millennium: The Aristocratic Presidencies 1900-1932
Pg 94

Chapter 7: The End of a Dream: The Dictatorship of General Martinez 1932-1944
Pg 119

Chapter 8: The Youth in Charge: The Beginning of the Juntas and Military Presidents
Pg 138

Chapter 9: Into the Abyss: The Civil War 1979-1992
Pg 155

Chapter 10: A New Beginning and the end of the Colon: Peace and Globalization in the 21st Century
Pg 165

Chapter 11: Collecting History
Pg 174

Chapter 12: 20th Century Coins by Decades
Pg 203

Bibliography Pg 247

Introduction

On January1, 2001, part of the nation's heritage became a relic of history. The mighty dollar had replaced the age of the Colon in the 21st century. Decades of political and civil unrest had recently ended, thus allowing the nation to convert her currency to that of the dollar. It had taken El Salvador over 50 years to establish her own currency and it had been replaced in just a matter of months.

The history of the *colon* is one that needs to be told, since few people know little if anything about this nation's coins. This book will study the history of the national coins usage from the time it was a colony of Spain under the Guatemalan Kingdom to her status as a state in the Central American Federation all the way to her independence. El Salvador's lack of currency created a problem in terms of keeping a detailed record of what foreign currency or goods were used as legal tender during the early years of the republic.

Therefore, as much as I have tried to verify the existence of foreign currency in the country, there is a good likelihood that numerous international coins were used as tender that we have no record of. Furthermore, I couldn't write this book without briefly going over the political history of the country, since politics determined economic policy.

Why was Colon the adopted currency name? Where was the national mint located? When were the first colones minted? Why did it take so long to establish a national currency? I hope to address and answer these and many other questions that the reader might have.

CHAPTER 1: BACK IN THE DAYS:

THE KINGDOM OF GUATEMALA UNDER SPANISH RULE

Planting the Seeds:
The Kingdom of Guatemala and The Federal Republic of Central America

The nation we call El Salvador was discovered by Spain in 1524. Like most nations in Latin America, El Salvador was settled and colonized by the Spanish. The Spanish crown decided to divide the Latin American colonies by region with each being controlled by a vice regent or governor. The three regions in Latin America were divided as follows: the vice regent of Mexico, the vice regent of Guatemala and the vice regent of Peru. El Salvador at the time was called San Salvador and was under the control of the vice regency of Guatemala which controlled Central America Each region was governed by rules established by the crown, but enforced by each vice regent. All three vice regents had established mints to cover each regions currency needs. The seat of power in Central America was Guatemala and a mint was built there for the purpose of minting currency for the region.

Vice Regent of Guatemala Mint

As we have briefly discussed, the vice regency of Guatemala was in charge of minting coins for use in Central America, with the region's mint being established in Guatemala. Several coins were produced during the time in this mint, which was chartered in 1600 and function till 1801.

Independence

As Spain's influence started to fall in the region many states took up the cause of independence and together they advocated their right for self rule. The first two decades of the 19th century were chaotic for Spain. With Spain's army and navy being stretch to the point of breaking, the states that composed the Kingdom of Guatemala declared their independence on September 12, 1821 without a single shot being fired.

Mexican Empire under Emperor Agustín de Iturbide

Independence came without a fight in the Central American region of the Spanish empire. Spain was too busy fighting the Mexican revolutionaries and other revolutionaries in South America to give the Central American region any importance.

The states in the vice regency declared their independence once they saw that Spain was too weak and that local Spanish authorities would pose no resistance. On September 15, 1820 all states in Central America declared their independence from Spain without as much as firing single shot.

CHAPTER 2: A UNITED FRONT: THE CENTRAL AMERICAN FEDERATION

The Central American Federation

Independence from Spain was short lived when General Iturbide obtained power in Mexico. He planned to annex Central America into his empire. From the beginning, the Central American states were not unified in supporting a free state. Instead, personal greed convinced many conservatives and former royalists to join Mexico. Many of the supporters hailed from Guatemala, the former center of power in the region. Although San Salvador wanted to remain independent and put up a good fight against Iturbide's forces, the state fell into Iturbide's hands.

The empire Iturbide created lasted only a couple of months, and by 1823 he was overthrown. His armies in Central America, led by General Filisola, decided to return home. However, before Filisola left, he gathered all the leaders of the region and encouraged them to form a united government. Filisola even decided to delay his departure, so that a peaceful conference could debate the structure of the new nation.

The federation was finally established in November of 1824 when a constitution was finally agreed upon by the states. Two Salvadorians Jose Arce and Juan Villacorte were part of a three man executive committee that ran the young nation.

The federation would consist of three branches of government; executive, legislative and judicial. Much of the inspiration for the new constitution came from the USA's constitution. However, the weakness of the Federation's constitution reflected more the original articles of confederation with a weak executive branch.

The majority of the delegation of the Central American Federation wanted a strong government, but deeply feared a strong executive or dictator. In creating a sub-par constitution, the thought process was that the document would be revised in the near future, however, the constitution was needed to establish the new nation.

The Federation established the absolute right to mint coins in the nation on March 3, 1824. Furthermore, the new laws forbade any Spanish emblems on currency and established the design of the federation's coins. Unfortunately, the use of several foreign coins and counterfeit currency made regulating money difficult.

The manufacturing of coins would be delegated to the three states that had the capacity and equipment to mint the federation's currency. Those three states where: Guatemala, Costa Rica and Honduras.

The lion's share of coins were produced by Guatemala; since that state had the experience of minting coins for the Kingdom of Guatemala and had the necessary experience and equipment to continue the job. The state of Costa Rica followed in production while Honduras was dead last in production. The fact that El Salvador did not establish a mint would become an issue when later in the decade scarcity of the federation's coins would lead to El Salvador accepting foreign coins and establishing laws to fight counterfeiting.

By October 1824, the newly established Central American Federation would crack down on counterfeiters and would agree to ban counterfeit coins in the new federation. The use of counterfeit currency was a problem, particularly when we discuss cobs that were irregularly shaped and worn out due to decades of use in the region.

An Imperfect Alliance

The state of El Salvador would not only suffer a lack of coin shortages because of the lack of a mint, but the various armed conflicts would alienate her from aid from neighboring states. The state became used to various civil wars and armed conflicts from the decision taken from the various state governments that constantly established new alliances and that were led by various governors.

The state of El Salvador found herself between 1829 and 1841 in seven different armed conflicts that saw her battling her neighbors over different political issues. Throughout much of this period, the federal government saw its power decline leading to states pursuing and seeking a greater autonomy in their decisions; thus all but nailing the coffin on the federations existence.

The first political problem the nation would encounter was with its first elections for president. Instead of a popular vote deciding the winner, the legislation ultimately decided to elect Jose Arce even though he had lost the popular vote. Needless to say, the controversy made selecting a cabinet impossible, since many of the intellectual elites had opposed or ran against Arce.

The second problem, the young nation had, was in how the checks and balances ultimately kept government from functioning at all. The president had no veto power.

This was due to the fear of many Central Americans of a dictatorship that could be easily established in the young nation. Thus, President Arce had no cabinet or real power to set his agenda in motion. The president was just a figurehead.

The legislative branch was by design the most powerful branch of government. It consisted of a congress and a senate. The congress was made up of population representation and was in charge of making laws. The senate was composed of two men from each state having the duties of either passing or rebuking congressional laws. Furthermore, it decided constitutional issues. Overall a two thirds majority was needed to pass laws.

Here, the biggest problem was in how congress assigned congressmen by representation. The almost universal fear of Guatemala among the other four states kept the federation from supporting or enforcing bills. The fear was indeed justified, since the Guatemalan state held the most pro-monarchist and financial elite citizens of the federation. These Guatemalan politicians wanted a weak federal government in order to protect their own interests. The Guatemalan elites would indeed play a pivotal and devastating role in the breakup of the federation.

The judicial branch was by far the weakest branch of government. It was almost non- existed. Many of its decisions were neither enforced nor publicized to the general public. Needless to say that as soon as the civil war started the court stopped functioning.

We can conclude that the first year of the federation was a bad start to the young nation, but it also reflected the chaotic atmosphere in government that ultimately doom any union.

Types of Coins Minted by the Federation

The federation's mints were efficient in producing gold coins that paid for large investments throughout the existence of the federation. Unfortunately, the production of smaller denominations of silver coins would become scarcer as the federation started to disintegrate. This problem would have an adverse effect throughout the nation, and in states like El Salvador, where most transactions were done via smaller denominations, as the lack of currency made trade much more difficult and coins scarcer.

Examples: a first set of silver and gold CAM coins from 1824

Arce's downfall and Morazán's rise

El Salvador had two important leaders in the federal government. First, it had Bishop Delgado a man who had fought for independence twice against Spain and Mexico. For his leadership skills he was elected as president of the federal congress. It also had a fellow Salvadorian in Arce as President of the Federation. However, by 1826, many Salvadorians started getting worried that Arce was alienating the other states in the federation and strengthening his grip on power. That year Arce imprisoned the Guatemalan governor and built a federal army. Soon Arce was involved in a civil war fighting all political sides. The war would last three years, while it wouldn't inflict major losses; it weakened all branches of federal government and strengthened each state government.

During this period, a young politician and soldier from Honduras rose up the ranks to become the leader of all liberal causes in Central America. That man was named Francisco Morazán.

General Morazán's Presidency and the First Provisional Salvadorian Coins

Politics, as usual, played a major role in the Federation's eventual failure as a nation. Politics between conservatives and liberal factions of each state would bring upon the first armed conflict in the young nation's history in 1828. Unfortunately, for the state of El Salvador, she would be the battleground for the civil war that would bring General Morazán to power.

During 1828, the state found itself surrounded by the threat of invasion by the federal government who was strongly influenced by the conservatives in the state of Guatemala. In didn't take long for the federal government to decide to influence San Salvador by using force.

The state of El Salvador did not hesitate to seek assistance from the most powerful liberal governor in Honduras' General Morazán to come to her aid. During this era the liberal government of El Salvador was led by Mariano Prado who decided to acquire all the states precious assets in order to fund the war until General Morazán could relieve the state.

Samples: 1828 and 1829 Provisional coins

Guatemala, the Federation's capital, had been governed by a conservative faction since her independence from Spain. The conservative faction in other states was nowhere as strong as in Guatemala. Liberals for the most part controlled the other four member states for much of the federation's history.

In 1829, after years of Guatemalan influence, General Morazán invaded the nation's capital and took power shortly after. President Morazán would rule the country for the next 11 years until he was overthrown in battle in 1838.

Prado Coins

With the threat of invasion by the federal government, the governor of the state of El Salvador, Mariano Prado prepared the state for an invasion and the start of civil war.

One of the ideas of the Prado government was to pass legislation that would acquire excessive silver and gold decorations and jewelry from all churches in the state for the purpose of melting them and converting them to coins.

The coins minted during this time would become known as Prado provisional coins and they would become the first provisional coins minted. Furthermore, author J Roberto Jovel points out that because the coins were minted under siege in a plaza where the federal government was attacking the state, that these coins are obsidian (minted under a direct siege). Thus, making them the only obsidian coins ever minted in Central America.

The state set up an emergency mint in the capital to manufacture coins for the state during the war. These coins were made by manual equipment and were pretty much rudimentary in quality. The coins were made from such bad quality silver that many broke or chipped away after being used just a few times.

As the war continued and Morazán's forces repelled the federal forces and pushed toward Guatemala, the Prado government came to an end. New elections were held in 1829 and Jose Maria Cornejo became the new governor by popular vote.

Cornejo's government would inherit a government overburdened with debt and no real investments or options to raise funds. Throughout, his tenure, the government would impose new taxes on anything of value in order to raise funds to pay up debt and to fund new projects.

During Cornejo's government a number of changes would take place that would impact the state's currency for better or worse. The first major change came in 1830 when news that several four reales pieces in circulation were suspected of being counterfeit. The government passed legislation outlawing all four reales pieces from circulating in 1830. Having ban the use of the four reales and fearing more counterfeiting, the government, later that year, decided to insure the authenticity of currency by countermarking each coin in circulation. In reality, only the capital coins were countermarked and some even circulated with no sign engraved on them.

By early 1829, Morazán's main army defeated Arce's federal troops thus ending Arce's grip on power. Senator Jose Barrundia was placed as the temporary president until elections could be held in 1830. Morazán's popularity was enough for him to easily win the presidency later that year.

Morazán, it can be argued, has been Central America's greatest leader. Without a doubt, his personal beliefs inspired all states in the federation to achieve their best or at least to dream big. Morazán's progressive beliefs were ahead of their time.

For example, Morazán believe in universal education and limiting the Catholics church's influence in the nation. These policies would make him an easy target for conservatives who wanted to derail any idea of progress that would endanger either their land or political stability.

Morazán increased his military support while at the same time he helped establish a strong base of liberal politicians in every state. However, as early as 1831 he was challenged by dissidents led by former president Arce.

The Salvadorian governor at the time, Jose Maria Cornejo, was convinced by Arce to secede from the federation and by proclamation the governor did so. Arce was trying to destabilize the Morazán administration by having several armed skirmishes throughout the federation at the same time San Salvador seceded from the country. Ultimately, the secession was crushed.

Countermark 1830

The year 1830 is important for the numismatics history of El Salvador as it marks the first time that the state minted her own coins. In this case they were provisional coins.

The countermark would compromise a small block with a volcano and the initials S on each side of the volcano with a date of 1830 on the bottom of the volcano. The S.S represented the city of San Salvador, while the volcano represented the national emblem.

Re-establishment of circulation for all silver coins

In October 1830 the state again passed new laws that would alleviate the markets shortages of coins. The new laws re-established the acceptance in the market of all silver coins. Furthermore, it set up stiff financial fines for merchants and government agents who would refuse to accept any silver currency as payment.

Several political skirmishes between 1831 and 1832 between the federal government and the state, mostly over taxes, caused the state of San Salvador to increase taxes to pay off her debt. By 1832 the federal government had decided to move the capital to San Salvador. President Morazán had two reasons why he chose to move the capital. The first being that the state of El Salvador had been the most vocal in opposing resources being drained from the state, leading to political unrest against the federal authorities in 1832. The second reason for Morazán to transfer the federal capital was to reduce the influence of the conservative movement still strong in Guatemala.

Nevertheless, the Cornejo government was shocked over what it perceived as a violation of her sovereign rights and immediately re-established the army to fight what they perceived was another invasion by the federal government.

Cornejo Provisional Coins

Because of this threat to the state, the Cornejo government re-established a provisional mint in 1832 to fund the war. All coins minted during this armed conflict would be known as Cornejo provisional coins. The new coins retained much of the similarities of the Prado provincial coins years earlier with some differences.

Unlike the variety of different coins minted in 1828, the Cornejo government would only produce a two reales coin in silver. Again the manufacturing took place in the capital of San Salvador.

Return of Governor Prado

The war lasted a couple of months, but General Morazán was successful in beating the forces of governor Cornejo. As a result, former governor Prado once again became governor in 1832 after the federal government successfully squashed the Cornejo government's army and ousted him from office.

One of the first policies the new administration took was to cut expenses and find ways to increase the state's coffers. Therefore, on August 1832, the legislation approved laws that would recognize the provincial coins of 1828 and 1832 and all federal currency as legal tender in the state.

The President's Dilemma

The biggest threat to the Morazán administration was without a doubt the Catholic Church and her loyal conservative political base. This political alliance made reforms almost impossible to pass through the congress or to enforce in individual states.

The federation was constantly battling armed skirmishes throughout the federation and President Morazán appeared more interested in squashing these militias than in running the country. Much to the resentment of President Morazán, the people began comparing him to his predecessor President Arce for failing to institute much needed reforms.

Dealing with political adversaries obviously made every president unpopular, as all of them were distracted from instituting reforms. Whoever was in power was in essence paranoid by what his adversaries would do to displace him and therefore afraid to propose any real reform.

Many states by the early 1830's, wanted reform and a stronger constitution that was supposed to make the government work. All states contributed tax money and raw materials to the federal government, but they didn't get much in return for supporting the federal government.

An important decision was made in the early 1830's when the federal capital was finally transferred from Guatemala City to Sonsonate and then to its permanent place in San Salvador. The fear of a powerful Guatemalan elite competing or influencing the federal administration finally convinced Morazán to transfer his capital headquarters.

Although, the constitution never referred to a permanent establishment for a federal capital, Morazán decided it was time to establish one outside of Guatemala. The move didn't gain Morazán many friends, if anything it weakened Morazán's influence.

The San Martin Government and Meddling by General Morazán

Unpopular policies that raised taxes and fees by the Prado administration led to various uprisings throughout the state that forced Prado to resign and have his vice governor Joaquin de San Martin take over as governor. The federal government did not recognize San Martin and expected Prado to resume power.

When Prado refused to return, the federal government decided to invade the state. Although, San Martin would win election the next year, the federal government never recognized San Martin as governor. During these hostile times, the San Martin government would re-establish a provisional mint to aid in not only paying her current debts, but also to prepare for the upcoming war with the federal government.

The San Martin Provisional Coin

In 1833, the new provisional coins started to circulate in the market. The one real coin would be the only provisional coin minted in 1833 and it would offer several new characteristics that her predecessors lacked. The coin would for the first time include the full name of the state and include the national seal.

Due to weak materials in the coins, like the previous Prado coins, the coins were constantly breaking or chipping apart. Therefore, new coins were minted with several variations in the legend area. The last variation of coins would include the one Real and two Reales minted in silver.

The Morazán Puppet Governors

By 1834, Morazán had defeated San Martin and had replaced him with several governors. Elections were held in 1834 with the winners being Dionisio Herrera as governor and Jose Maria Silva as vice governor. Herrera, for political reasons, would decline his post, thus making Silva the new governor.

During the Silva administration a growing concern over the increasing number of counterfeit coins was spreading throughout the state. A number of counterfeit reports caused many merchants throughout the state to demand foreign or federal coins instead of provisional coins. The government responded by passing new laws to punish counterfeiters and by countermarking coins in the market.

Shortage of coins throughout the state

The state of El Salvador ran into trouble with the lack of currency circulating in the state throughout much of the federation's period. At some point, the state government decided that no matter how many coins they imported there was still going to be a shortage of coins in the market. Thus, the state government decided to come up with some unique and creative ways to legalize foreign currency and created laws to protect the few federation coins in circulation.

Counter Stamps

Throughout much of the 19th century, El Salvador would use a counter stamp on foreign coins in circulation in the country. The counter stamp, in El Salvador's case, consisted of a small national emblem engraved on the face of any foreign coins circulated in the country.

A great number of counter-stamped coins are graded low due to the great wear these coins have had and the fact that many of them are the only samples known to have been counter stamped with the national emblem. It should also be noted that it would not surprise experts to see new foreign coin specimens since a great number of these coins are scarce.

Not all foreign coins were counter-stamped and many circulated and were accepted as currency by many merchants throughout the state and throughout the federation. Both government officials and merchants welcomed the additional foreign currency. It seemed that it temporarily addressed the shortages of coins. However by accepting coins from other countries and from older periods it introduced a number of counterfeit coins to the state's economy.

Counterfeits became a major problem throughout the state during the late 1830's forcing the state to impose new legislation to deal with counterfeiters. New legislation was drafted as a result of a growing backlash by merchants who were becoming skeptical of the precious metal contents of some coins produced in the state as well as foreign coins. The state promoted the new laws by advertising rewards not only for counterfeit coins, but also for people who turn in a possible counterfeiter. Penalties were imposed on both people using known counterfeit coins and the counterfeiters themselves. Penalties ranged from fines to imprisonment.

Zigzag Countermarks

Although laws were proposed against counterfeiters and enacted, the problem still persisted in the early 1830's. The state decided to mark coins. The obvious reasons for this were to first reassure merchants that the value of coins in the market was legitimate and to finally stamp out counterfeit coins from the state. The government of Governor Jose Maria Silva (1834-1835) enlisted a decree during Mid-December of 1834 that established the method and regulations that local municipalities would use to test each provisional coin in their community.

The laws also went one step further in admonishing the people into accepting the provisional coins or otherwise they would risk being fined twice the value of the coins they rejected. In essence, the government would do whatever was needed to ensure the use of the provisional coins, and enforce the acceptance of the coins on the citizens.

The state came up with a simple way of testing coins by late 1834 and that was to impose a mark on each coin by sawing the coin enough to test its metal content. The purpose of sawing the coin was to make sure that the coin's metal content was silver and not cooper. If the coin was silver, than the coin was given back to the citizen with an apparent mark on its face. When the coin was proven to be mostly cooper, then the tester would cut the coin in half and give back the two halves to the person whom had brought the coin for testing.

Coins with such a saw mark became known as zig zag countermark coins and were commonly used throughout the state and the federation. The state unfortunately, could not force out all counterfeit coins. As a result, the state ended testing coins pinning its hopes on stronger anti-counterfeiting laws.

Example: Peru-Bolivia coin with zig zag mark from the saw

The state continued to request assistance from the federal government in solving her lack of currency. The state also discontinued use of certain coins that were deemed to be easily counterfeited.

Morazán runs for re-election

By the time of the presidential elections of 1834, Morazán was not a popular president. Though he ran for a second term he lost the election to Senator Valle. Due to a medical illness, Senator Valle died before he could assume office. What would have become of the Federation under Valle as President is a great "what if" of history. As a result of Valle's death, the Federation organized a run off of the remaining candidates. President Morazán won the majority of votes and was re-elected.

Possible Mint

By 1835 El Salvador was seriously considering building a mint in order to provide fractional currency that was scarce and needed for day-to-day activities. The Silva government received federal support in the quest to acquire both machinery and knowledge from the federation's main mint in Guatemala City.

The Guatemalan government after several communications decided to help the state by providing the necessary equipment and experts in the field. Unfortunately, the Guatemalan authorities could never provide the necessary equipment or experts needed to start a mint in El Salvador. This was due to a combination of economic and political uncertainties in Guatemala at that time. As a result, talks broke down and the federal government in July 1835 officially notified the state of Guatemala that no further action was to be taken to assist the state of El Salvador in building a mint.

Espinoza Provisional Coins

By mid-1835, the state was being run by a new governor in Nicolas Espinoza whom would govern for a couple of months before being deposed by the federal government. During his brief stint, he would re-establish the provisional mint in order to produce scarce coins that the state was lacking. The provisional coins minted in 1835 would all consist of silver and would have values of one-half Real and one Real.

By late-1835, the government of El Salvador, after much debate, decided to withdraw all provisional coins in the state. There are two main reasons why the state decided to act. The first being, that although the currency minted was provisional and only for use within the state, it was also occasionally being used in neighboring states. The governments of those states did not appreciate the lack of precious metal content of coins used in El Salvador nor the simplistic design that led it to be easily counterfeited. Therefore, various governments decided to ban the use of provisional coins from El Salvador in their markets and to have them either melted or re-minted by their mint. The second reason why the state of El Salvador would withdraw the provisional coins was that their simple design was increasing the number of counterfeit money, thus risking the financial integrity of the state.

The state of San Salvador would fight counterfeiters with the first penal code aimed solely at counterfeiters and known associates of the trade. These laws would set forth punishment through hard labor and stiff fines when any attempt to counterfeit the nations provisional currency was found.

The first provisional coins to get banned were the most recent provisional coins the San Martin series of 1835. The simple design and lack of much silver content (compared to her predecessors) created uncertainly within the market, so much so, that many merchants would come to refuse the currency while others would only accept each coin below face its face value.

The government decided to do away with this series on February 14, 1835 by attrition. Slowly, people would be able to pay their bills without having to trade or lose the value of the currency. The government though, became concerned that too many San Martin coins were on the market therefore it decided to cease recognizing the series as legitimate currency in the market by June 9 1836.

Ban on Provisional coins

By mid-1835 the federal government had decided that all provisional currency in both El Salvador and Honduras was not only easy to counterfeit throughout the federation, but that the existence of authentic provisional coins were illegal. The various provisional coins in El Salvador had been below silver content and of reduced weight, a violation of the federal constitution. The federal government recalled these coins and had them re-minted by the federal mint.

Even though the federal government was now aiding the state of El Salvador in minting federal coins, the state was still in short supply of all fractional currency. The federal government would ask the Guatemalan government for a loan to cover the shortage of currency and would even enter into a business transaction with private entrepreneurs to acquire some currency for the state.

The fast conversion of provisional coins to standard federal coins was hailed as a victory by the Morazán federal government. Many hope that the influx of standard coins would suffice the market and finally end the shortage of currency in the state.

The Federations Decline

By 1835, the congress was finally able to meet and discuss constitutional reform. However, the 1835 Federal constitution left everyone feeling left out. The constitution failed to address reforms from taxes to the establishment of a federal seat of power. The only good amendment was the freedom of religion clause that overturned the Catholic only faith clause of 1825. In essence, the new constitution was pointless and many states started to openly question the existence of a federal government that taxed and demanded so much, but in return offered little services to the states.

After the failure of the 1835 constitution and the re-election of Morazán, the conservatives started to organize around a young Guatemalan soldier by the name of Rafael Carrera. Most of Carrera's support came from native Indians and conservatives politicians who felt they needed a military man to match Morazán. By the late 1830's Carrera was the most dangerous man in the federation.

The general ignorance of the Guatemalan peasants along with their religious ideology made them a powerful base for the conservative politicians to exploit. It became easy for the conservative elite to blame the president for a variety of ailments ranging from lack of clean water to the spread of cholera.

The end approaching

Although the breakup of the federation would take a few more years by 1838 the federation had collapsed after various state legislations had decreed that the federation was not in their interest. The Costa Rican assembly gathered to discuss the situation in the country and concluded that the new federal constitution of 1835 was never really ratified by the state and therefore it didn't recognize the federal government or the Federation. This declaration of cessation was not met by force. Instead, the President ignored this declaration thinking that once he defeated Carrera's army and supporters he could rein in the remaining states.

Clearly, Morazán had underestimated the unpopularity of his government. As soon as Costa Rica announced its intention of seceding the remaining states followed suit .By 1839, only El Salvador remained a member of the Federation. Even in El Salvador, Morazán didn't enjoy overwhelming popular support and he was soon becoming a liability.

Problems with Supporting Morazán

The state of El Salvador would continue to suffer shortages in currency in 1839.Unforunately, no longer could the state depend on federal coins from member states and had to manage the few resources it had. To make matters worse in February 1839 both Nicaragua and Honduras would join forces in an attempt to overthrow the Morazán government. The war lasted 11 months, but would drain the state's coffers. The state would also suffer when an uprising took place in the capital in September by forces united against Morazán and aided by Guatemala. Lastly, an earthquake rocked the state the following month after the uprising was squashed. With all these political and natural problems, the state sought new ways of issuing currency.

Peruvian-Bolivian Federation Coins

The short lived Peruvian-Bolivian confederation coins made their way through the ports of the state and would find them spreading throughout the state. Many merchants would not accept the coins at face value and many would reject them entirely. Naturally, the government's response was to ban them from all the market in order to eliminate any confusion or counterfeit problems.

Under the enormous political and financial pressures, the state of El Salvador would seek to legalize the Peruvian-Bolivian coins, but only after finding out whether their silver content was up to standard with the federation's guidelines. The state would seek the assistance of the Guatemalan mint in analyzing the metal content of these coins. Although the two countries were at odds politically, the Guatemalan mint saw the importance of the study and promptly analyzed the coins.

Having determine that a great number of coins were indeed up to standard, the state decided to established laws in order for them to become legal tender. By the federation's guidelines, the majority of the coins were deemed to be authentic. However, coins that fell short of the government's silver content were called fake. Therefore, laws needed to be created in order to allow these coins to circulate freely in the market.

Most merchants, however, were not willing to accept the coins, so in order to entrust confidence in the state, the federal government would countermark each coin that was up to federation standards.

Sample: *A classic 1838 Sur Peru Coin*

The 1839 Countermark

Although the coins would begin to be countermarked in 1840, the seal bares the year of 1839. Several currencies would be countermarked, such as the:

- two Reales Lima 1825-1836

- one half Real from Chile.

The seal of the countermark is simple. It includes the national emblem (volcano) and 1839 underneath the volcano, all enclosed in a square.

The End of Morazán and the Federation

President Morazán's term expired in 1839 and no intentions were made in calling for elections for a nation that no longer existed. Once Morazán's term expired he became the governor of El Salvador and created a new army to both defend the state from invasion and to invade Guatemala and capture Carrera.

By 1840, Morazán decided to invade Guatemala in order to restore his political allies who had been deposed by General Carrera. A few months later, Morazán failed to achieve victory in Guatemala and was forced to retreat. Morazán instead chose to voluntarily go into self exile, all but ending the existence of the federation.

New Laws for Foreign Coins in Circulation

The new governor of El Salvador, Norberto Ramirez, would seek to again address the shortages of currency in the state by addressing the legality of various South American coins in circulation that had not been addressed by previous administrations. It was decided that the state would legalize the acceptance of these coins and set up stiff penalties for merchants who chose not to accept these coins. For example, rejection of the coins carried a fine of five pesos and anywhere between five and 10 days in jail. The government therefore, hope that legalizing all proper currency circulating in the state would cut down on counterfeiters.

Morazán's Death

Although, Morazán would return in 1843 to Costa Rica and become the president of the country he was overthrown as soon as people found out that he wanted to build an army and go after Carrera again in the hope of re-establishing the federation. He was tried and executed by Costa Rican authorities in 1843. Thus, this ended the life of one of Central America's greatest patriots.

A New Beginning

The state of El Salvador unfortunately had to deal with the perception that it had always supported Morazán when it came to having ties with sister nations. However, in 1840 the state declared its independence again, but this time as a sovereign nation.

For the next several decades the young nation of El Salvador would struggle to maintain its independence from Guatemala's Carrera who by default became the most influential dictator in the region for decades to come. The young state of El Salvador from now on would determine her own destiny and be judged by her actions as an independent sovereign state.

CHAPTER 3 INDEPENDENCE AT LAST: THE STATE 1840-1880

The Early Republican Years 1840-1900

Shortly after the federation's fall, new currencies from various nations would circulate in the new nation as legal tender. The state, during the Federal years had constantly depended on foreign coins to satisfy its needs. Nothing would really change in the new nation of El Salvador as the use of foreign coins would continue. As the coffee exports grew by the mid-1800's the nation for the first time would see many plantation owners experiment with the idea of paying employees with tokens from their own estate.

In fact, what constituted legal tender was debatable among individual citizens. The government would allow the use of certain coins and would use legislative laws and decrees to enforce acceptance of coins that the private sector had refused to accept due to concerns over the quantity of silver.

Yet, throughout the next decade's laws would either not be enforced or be so lax that individuals still would decide whether or not to accept any coins they distrusted as being counterfeit or lacking in silver content. Not all transactions in the young nation would be paid via coins; there is enough evidence to believe that many people used cocoa beans and even eggs as currency. Not untill the Central American Mint LTD started producing national coins in the late 19th century would the practice of bartering start winding down.

Testing the Market

The new nation would keep the same standards when it came to accepting or possibly minting silver and gold coins that the old Federations had. However, determining what each foreign coin was worth was the challenge.

One of the new coins in circulation was the Spanish pesetas that feature Queen Isabel II. The new coin brought a degree of suspicion, since few knew whether the coin met the standards the nation imposed on silver coins. Therefore on October 18, 1845 President Joaquin Guzman banned all these pesetas from circulating as legal tender in the country. Further studies showed that they indeed didn't meet the legal requirement.

The lack of coins in the market and the banning of the new pesetas made coins scarcer in the new republic. The abundance of coins from other nations and the availability of provincial coins that were banned under the 1835 government degree led the government of President Dr. Eugenio Aguilar to re-establish these silver coins as legal tender.

The legislative actions to countermark existing coins to insure the silver content did not solve the nation's shortages of coins. Efforts were made to establish a mint.. The first serious attempt by the sovereign country to establish a mint occurred in 1847 when President Aguilar approved a proposal from the Anglo-Salvadorian mining company to establish a mint in the capital. The proposal drew scrutiny over fears that what was considered a national obligation was going to branch out exclusively to the private sector. Because of these concerns the legislative branch never ratified the proposal and the proposal died soon after.

Nevertheless, in 1852 under a new President Doroteo Vasconcelos, the government would renew the idea of establishing a mint via a public-private partnership. Alas, this proposal also went nowhere and the idea of establishing a mint would not be entertained for a few years.

The gold rush in California and the increase in trade led to an increase of American coins in the nation around the late 1840's. The American coins were different in terms of silver content and in denominations which once again caused confusion among the people who were used to pesetas and pesos.

The government quickly saw the need for further coins that met the standards for silver and gold content and several American coins met those requirements. During several months in 1851 various legislative decrees were passed approving the circulation of American dollar coins and dimes in the country. Furthermore, the government imported several American dimes to deal with the ongoing shortages of small currency.

By the mid-1850's, the nation had such a great quantity of foreign coins that many merchants were rejecting coins from countries they did not trust with the silver or gold content. This of course created a major insecurity among the citizens who were paid in coins that their bosses deemed acceptable, but that could be rejected by individual merchants.

In order to solve this problem the government of President Rafael Juan Campo and Pomar created a table in 1856 that stated that all the known foreign currency in circulation in the country and their silver and gold content. The table was circulated throughout the country, so that the public would be aware of their existence and their values.

A renewed effort to fight counterfeiting was again taken up by the state when in 1857 the government started to inspect coins coming in from her ports after suspecting that illegal mints were abundant in neighboring Nicaragua. Once again, the state pledged to inspect and punish counterfeiters and their associates. However, counterfeiting would become a common problem throughout the country.

Gerardo Barrios

After years of being both a senator and a general of the army, Gerardo Barrios was elected president in 1859. President Barrios was a follower of the late General Morazán and his political agenda would be greatly influenced by the former President of the defunct Federation. His political influence would go beyond the nation's borders and would ultimately lead to political problems with neighboring Guatemala resulting in war.

Nevertheless, Gerardo Barrios would not only seriously start to address the nation's lack of currency, but would also be the first president in the nation's history to commission and appear in national coins.

Lack of coins was a recurrent problem that President Barrios felt needed to be addressed by asking for assistance from a nation that could help them establish a mint.

Guatemala, had the most experience in running a mint, so President Barrios felt that the neighboring state could help the nation establish a mint. Barrios would ask Guatemala to import silver and gold coins from Guatemala to keep up with demand for coins

that were up to the Salvadorian standards..
Nevertheless, the Salvadorian government
explored their options in establish a mint with the
private sector.

Possible Mints and the Barrios Coins

Of the various foreigners conducting business in the state was a business man named Sydney Oaksmith who came up with the idea of establishing a mint in San Salvador. The government granted Mr. Oaksmith the concession to establish a mint in early 1860. Sydney Oasksmith would in fact secure the necessary equipment for purchase in New York, but due to political and financial instability, the government could not provide the security nor the financial capital needed to purchase the machinery needed. The government though, felt that a new agreement could be made with a French financial powerhouse in, Emile Erlanger and Company, to establish a mint or acquire coins, but this also fell through due to the same financial and political issues Sydney Oaksmith faced earlier in the decade.

Gerardo Barrios Coins

President Gerardo Barrios was faced with an opportunity to mint Salvadorian coins with his image on them when a private citizen offered to create a few specimens for his approval. The president though felt he needed to have official coins minted from an

~ 51 ~

expert and in 1862 he would get the opportunity. The nation's ambassador to Turin, Italy had received a proposal from the Turin mint to mint Salvadorian coins. The president accepted the offer and the state of Turin would mint two coins; the 25 centavos and one Peso coins in 1862.

The coins produced would have the face of President Gerardo Barrios and the republic's name. The back would have the national emblem and show six volcanoes instead of the five that traditionally represented the five nations of Central America. Author J Roberto Jovel theorizes that the reason why six volcanoes appeared instead of five was not a mistake, but a desire of the President to re-established the old Central American Federation that included the short lived Los Altos state.

Sample: 1861 25 cent Barrios coin

The Guatemalan R Countermark

By late 1862, rumors were spreading throughout the nation's commercial centers that a majority of Guatemalan coins were counterfeited. As mentioned earlier, merchants had the opportunity to accept or deny coins even though the government had established rules and laws that forced citizens to accept all coins that the government had deemed were appropriate as legal tender. Unfortunately, like many laws, few were enforced by the appropriate authorities. The government feeling a sense that their support for these coins wasn't going to stop merchants from denying the acceptance of them, felt a need to issue a countermark for the Guatemalan coins.

The majority of coins from Guatemala that were countermarked were all the silver one half, one, two and four reales and one peso coins. The countermark chosen to distinguish these coins was unlike any the nation had ever struck. The countermark has an R letter that stands for "rehabilitated" surrounded by a circle that had anywhere between 20-21 small dots around the R mark.

Sample: Guatemalan real with 1862 "R" countermarked.

The End of President Barrios

President Gerardo Barrios, a loyal follower of General Morazán, and a man who wanted to re-established the Central American Federation would run into political problems with neighboring Guatemala in 1863. A war started after General Carrera invaded the country however the Salvadorians won the battle that resulted in a victory for Barrios. General Carrera was forced to retreat.

Unfortunately, for President Barrios, General Carrera again re-invaded the country months later and this time was successful in overthrowing Barrios from power. President Barrios would retreat to Nicaragua, but was captured in 1865 and was shortly executed as a traitor by his conservative enemies.

The new government that succeeded President Barrios was the conservative administration of Francisco Duenas in 1865. President Duenas turned out to be a moderately successful president in his term, but had little influence on monetary policy in the country during his administration. The Duenas administration would face the same problems with shortages of coins. Therefore, the Duenas administration decided in 1867 to accept foreign coins as payment for national debts and to create a list for all citizens to see the equivalent of foreign coins to Reales.

Tokens: "Owing one's soul to the company store"

It had been over 20 years since gaining independence and the state still didn't have a mint. In fact, the state had no real plans to mint any coins. The only coins minted were those by Gerardo Barrios earlier in the 1860's and those were of limited quantities.

As a result, most of the landowners and operators of large agricultural estates decided to create their own methods of paying their workers.

Sample: several tokens from different coffee fields

The usage of foreign silver and gold coins was scarce. The coins in circulation came from various nation's and their denominations and precious metal content differed. Although, the federal government tried to solve the issue with various countermarks and tables that showed metal content; the entire system, depended on merchants and citizens accepting foreign coins. In essence, the market determined value and acceptance.

Most of the country's citizens were peasants or farmers who depended on the big estates for work. Prior to the liberal reforms of the late 19th century, most native Indians lived with their families on community-owned land. As the main export for the country changed from indigo to coffee and as the government became more stable, the various administrations decided to privatize land for economic growth. The result was a huge surge in labor and a lack of land that forced many people to become laborers in estates that were once owned by their community.

The elite, knowing the difficulty of paying for goods, came up with the idea of paying workers with tokens early in the 1860's. No one can place the person or event that started the trend of paying workers via tokens, but soon all large estates would employ them over time.

The estates themselves would acquire these tokens from a number of foreign companies and some even manufactured them in their estates. According to Jose Arevalo, a number of San Francisco token manufacturers were responsible for the majority of these tokens in circulation. They were: Patrick and Co, C.A Klinter Co, L.H Moises Co and eventually Moises Klinker Co all manufacturing tokens for the big estates. Other tokens were produced by the French A. Popert de Paris and the German firm of W. Nathansen.

Most tokens in use were primarily for paying wages to workers. The token system operated very conveniently for the owner's advantage, for a number of reasons. First, all tokens were manufactured exclusively for a specific farm, thus tokens could only be redeemed in that estate. This obviously meant that workers had to redeem their tokens in the owner's private stores or in stores that had an agreement to redeem tokens for that particular estate. The employer in essence could control the cost and variety of goods that their own workers would purchase. Most goods were purchased by the owners at wholesale prices and then sold at retail prices to the workers. Secondly, the use of tokens controlled the number of workers that a farm could reliably expect to have on any given day. Ironically, the token system kept workers from leaving the estates, because few would dare risk going unemployed. It needs to be said, that many workers lived on the farms and were fed three meals a day and pretty much were taken care of by their bosses. The level of care and meals depended on the estate, but most estates only provided the bare minimum meals to survive and maintain a strong workforce. A third advantage in using tokens was that many estate owners used tokens not only as a means for payment, but as a means of control over the production of each worker.

For example, many tokens were engraved with particular tasks, such as *caballo* or horse which meant the workers had the duty to take use of a horse for an activity. A few tokens or even plates were created to identify an individual equivalent to a badge issue in offices today and these were used to supervise the workers' production in any given task.

The use of tokens also included those for rewards or specific goods. For example, a token with Agua could be redeemed for water. The exact amount or quality was not specified in the tokens themselves. A variety of tokens were actually produced domestically, others were foreign coins with the engraved initials of the farm or owner.

The use of tokens was never fully addressed by the federal government until the early 20th century. In fact, the issue of tokens was never taken up by the government until the administration of President Jorge Melendez in 1920. Accordingly, the administration wanted to create a new monetary policy and in doing so, on July 20, 1920, the government banned the use of tokens in the country. The use of tokens would continue due to the fact that the government was ill equipped in to enforce such laws and generally the law was pretty much discounted and ignored by the general population.

By the time of the coup that led to General Maximiliano Martinez to the presidency the nation was badly in need of a real monetary policy following the depression in the United States and depressed commodity prices of the major crops, such as coffee. On June 19, 1934 the central bank came into existence and with that all currency issued would fall under the responsibility of the central bank. The establishment of a central bank would essentially ban the use of tokens as payment, although limited use was still common in later years, for the most part the reform did away with the token system.

The last mention of tokens on any federal monetary policy occurred in 1961 when the Military-junta passed the nation's third monetary policy banning their use to compensate salaries.

The use of tokens, though widely used in Latin America and other nations struggling to establish their own mint, was used as currency in El Salvador throughout much of the 19th and early 20th century. It took the state over 50 years, to mint coins and to establish a mint and several more decades to actually enforce the monetary laws it had chosen to enact. Throughout the decades, a case can be made that a lack of national currency helped cement the great economic inequalities the nation, to this day, is still struggling to overcome.

There is no doubt in the author's mind that the token system was to no one's advantage, except for the plantation owners. The plantation owners could pay whatever they felt in salaries in simple metals that held absolutely no actual value outside the specific plantation and its stores. In rare situations, and if the owner had a previous agreement with a local merchant, tokens could be redeemed by the worker outside of the plantation. In essence, the workers became slaves to the owner's demands and wishes.

It's true that unlike slaves, they could leave the estate at will, but finding another job and traveling with a family was too much of a risk for the overall majority of workers. Many plantations gave their workers at least three meals a day plus shelter and clothing in exchange for their labor.

Accordingly, the owners of the farms could set the prices of goods sold by their stores and dictate how much food to give to their workers. Much like a public school, the owners educated and took care of their workers for better or worse. Thus the token system made the peasants children who needed to be taken care off .Many estates held big homes to shelter the many workers who would choose to live in the estates, since few had any money to pay for a home of their own.

Although the system of token usage is important to understand both the numismatic history and the overall economic history of El Salvador, few books exist today that cover this important aspect of the economy. The use of tokens in the country was widely used for several decades, but lack of interest by experts or lack of information, has unfortunately left this subject in the dark for far too long.

As far as research into Salvadorian tokens, there are only two known sources available to both collectors and historians that focus on tokens specifically for El Salvador. One is the unpublished work by Roberto Ulloa entitled the "*Tokens of El Salvador* "that focuses on all the known tokens and has a suggested list of prices for collectors to use as a guide. This work is a detailed study on the subject in terms of cataloging and pricing each token by plantation. Unfortunately, the author didn't write a historical account of tokens in general ,or of the plantations themselves, to help the collector understand each piece. Ultimately, Mr. Ulloa's unpublished work is a must for any collectors wishing to catalog Salvadorian tokens.

A recent work by Jose Cabrera entitled the *"Las Controversiales Fichas de Fincas Salvadorenas"* is the most concrete study on the subject by anyone interested in exonumia (the study of tokens). Cabrera addresses the issue of how and why tokens were use in the late 19th and early 20th century and sheds great light on questions of manufacturing and cost of tokens in general. Jose Cabrera's work is the most complete book on the history of tokens in El Salvador.

Countermark Coins

By 1868 the government would decide to re-examined all coins in order to make sure they weren't counterfeited. It was decided that a countermark would be inscribed into each coin to ensure its quality. The countermark would include the new national seal of which there are five different designs.

Sample: cob with 1868 countermarked

The goal of the countermark was both to distinguish worn out coins and withhold them from circulation and to make sure that the one and two reales coins had the equivalent silver content. Although, most coins with a countermark fit this description, not all of the coins countermarked should have been. There are various countermarked coins that had higher values. Apparently, the various government agents decided to countermark all coins they felt needed to be identified in order for the public to accept them.

By 1868, the government had decided to expand the countermark program to include various cob coins that were in circulation and had been rejected by citizens due to the wear and tear on them. The original legislative agreement called for all one Real cobs to be countermarked, but just like with coins previous marked, many cobs were countermarked due to the agent's independent decision that countermarking several cobs would increase the citizen's acceptance of them.

Nonetheless, most cobs that were countermarked were several hundred years old and many were so faded that very few features were visible to distinguish them from other cobs. The countermark would backfire, so by 1870 the government would consider the possibility of phasing out completely the use of cobs in the nation. This possibility also led the government to once again explore the idea of establishing a national mint.

Unfortunately, attempts to fade out cobs were never reached and the idea of establishing a new mint also faded from national debates as time progressed.

In 1872, the new liberal governments of El Salvador and Guatemala had signed a mutual peace agreement that led to both governments deciding to ban the use of cobs in both nations. The cob coins in El Salvador had always been mistrusted by the population, since a great number of them where counterfeited or were completely worn out.

Although, Guatemala had offered the Salvadorian government the opportunity to aid in the cost of withdrawing all cobs, political and natural disasters would make this agreement hard to successfully achieve in the short term. The Salvadorian government would fight an unexpected war against Honduras soon and experience an earthquake that would cripple the efforts of the government to focus on anything but reconstruction.

Countermarked of 1873

The abundance of English coins in the country made the government reconsider expanding its countermarked program to include British coins. So, in 1873 legislation was passed authorizing the use of the 1869 countermarked on various British coins.

Example of a British shilling with the 1869 countermark

Acquisitions of machinery for a mint

A curious event took place when both governments of El Salvador and Guatemala decided to invade Honduras then led by a conservative president Jose Maria Medina. The government of Honduras had petitioned the USA for machinery needed to improve their national mint, but due to the war the machinery was still in a Honduran port after being shipped from New York.

The port of Amapala was taken by Salvadorian troops in late 1873 and all possessions were transferred to El Salvador at the conclusion of the war. The machinery from the mint was part of the cargo acquired by the Salvadorian government that led many to believe that the government could finally established a mint from the confiscated machinery. However, several years of reconciliatory talks between the two governments after the peace accords led to the Salvadorian governments decision to return the equipment back as an act of good faith.

By 1875 the government of El Salvador would again be engaged in a new war with a border state, in this case it would be former allied Guatemala. The Salvadorian government would lose the war in a matter of months leading to a political shift back home that saw Rafael Zaldivar take over as president. Zaldivar, a liberal, would push a free a trade policy that would lead to the establishment of the nation's first bank and the first use of paper money in the country.

CHAPTER 4: THE BEGINNING OF THE LIBERAL STATE: LAND PRIVATIZATION AND THE CREATION OF THE MODERN STATE 1880-1892

Privatization of land 1870-1880

The nation had been ruled for years by a combination of either liberal or conservative presidents. However, the conservative party for years had a hold on power in the country whether it was in power or not due to the influence of Guatemala. General Rafael Carrera had dominated politics in Central America ever since the last days of the Federation and his successor Pedro de Aycinema continued his conservative policies.

Until the early 1870's the liberal Salvadorian presidents like Gerardo Barrios had run into direct military conflict with conservatives and their Guatemalan allies. The result was clear, liberal politicians who wanted to privatize Indian holdings could not. If they did, the liberal government risked a military conflict with Guatemala. Therefore, the native Indian population enjoyed overwhelming protection from the Catholic Church and from conservative landholders who were content with keeping the status quo.

The rise of liberal politicians in Guatemala in the late 1860's and their eventual presidential win in the 1870's brought overwhelming changes in El Salvador. The popularity of coffee plantations began in the mid 1850's, yet the biggest obstacle for the cultivation of coffee was the need for more land. Unfortunately, most of the desirable land needed to cultivate coffee in the 1860's was in the hands of the native Indian population. Thus, no liberal politician wanted to stir up trouble with these political conditions in the region.

Although President Barrios was overthrown and a conservative president in Francisco Duenas governed the country after 1865, Duenas governed much like Barrios. The biggest exception was that Duenas did go out of his way to protect and enhance the right of the native Indian population. President Duenas made no attempt to seize any land from Indians. He even squashed violent riots led by liberals with native Indian Salvadorian troops.

Furthermore, Duenas passed legislation giving the Indians equal representation in congress. Overall, Francisco Duenas governed like the typical conservative president of the era.

The loss of a strong Guatemalan conservative base led to Col. Santiago Gonzalez leading a coup to overthrow President Francisco Duenas in early 1871. Finally, the liberal movement could finally propose their agenda and one of the first items on their agenda was to privatize all land controlled by the Indian communities.

Although the Indian population revolted with the assistance of the Catholic Church months after Duenas was overthrown in San Miguel they were quickly put down by the new modernized army. In fact, the San Miguel riots would be the largest and last act of disobedience to at least threaten the liberal establishment for years to come until 1932.

It took the coffee planters and their liberal allies several years to finally propose legislation to abolish communal properties. By 1881, the legislative body passed the country's sweeping land reform. The new law gave property owners a certain time period to claim land and apply for title. Those who didn't claim their land would lose it to the government or a prospector.

Those that benefited in purchasing or even, in some cases, stealing the land were the growing coffee farmers that now had better lands to plant coffee crops. The indigo crop, that once was the economic lifeline of the economy, was slowly being discontinued for a newer more profitable crop (coffee) that required more labor and more land. The land reform of 1881 was the foundation for the socio-political system the country would endure for the next 100 years.

With the land reforms in place, the liberals now set their sights on finally instituting and establishing a mint in the country. With so much land for sale, the country needed to establish its own currency. The first step the liberals took toward establishing a mint was to write a set of monetary laws in which the state could set up the denominations of coins and the amount of precious metal content in them. Finally, the state took the ideas of establishing a mint seriously by not just proposing a plan, but by actually writing laws to regulate the new currency.

The nation would still facilitate the use of foreign coins as it had done before due to the lack of coins in the country during the time of President Zaldivar. By the 1870's Honduran and Mexican coins were the most common coins in circulation in the country. These coins would be examined and authorized as legal tender to circulate in the country. In the case of Honduran coins, the peace deal between the two countries brought a level of cooperation in dealing with counterfeiters fleeing the state of Honduras and into El Salvador.

By 1877, the government would authorize for the first time the use of paper money as legal tender. By 1880, the government would welcome the first private bank, Banco Internacional del Salvador into existence in the country. The new bank not only would establish the credit all the landowners and merchants needed for commerce, but it also would become the first entity to issue paper money shortly after its founding.

First Monetary Laws

The issue of what to do with cobs again was brought up by the Zaldivar government who felt that the use of paper money and increase in foreign coins, during his period would solve the shortages of coins. Therefore, the government in 1880 decided to do away with cobs and finally replaced them with coins.

Once again though, the government failed to understand the need for a permanent replacement of cobs, since most small transactions could not deal with paper money or foreign silver and gold coins. It meant that the market needed small coin denominations to circulate freely, the job cobs fulfilled this need. The Zaldivar government did not stop the withdrawal of cobs, but instead authorized the use of stamps to fulfill the need of not having small denominations coins. Stamps became a new way for the liberal government to try to establish a mint and at the same time phase out an antiquated system.

By 1882, the government of President Zaldiva decided to write the nations first monetary laws. It was evident that the nation was now finally better off than decades prior. The use of foreign coins and the authorization of paper money along with stamps brought the Zaldiva government closer to establishing a mint for the country.

The government was determined to seek and buy the necessary equipment needed to establish a mint. The government, in the meantime, created a chart of all available foreign coins in circulation and wrote the equivalent precious metal content of these coins compared to old federation coins that were still in circulation. The government was clearly cataloging and monitoring the use of foreign coins in the country.

In 1885, General Francisco Menendez staged a coup and became president. During his reign, several events would take place that would finally lead the nation towards establishing a mint of its own.

1889 Birmingham Issue

The lack of small denominations had been an ongoing issue for the nation since its founding. The previous administrations had failed to solve this problem and it seemed that the nation was stuck using whatever it could as currency. Politics was usually the culprit behind the many proposed laws for either minting or establishing a mint that were usually derailed when compromises could not be established between the governing political parties. The Menendez administration faced the same political deadlock as past administrations, when it proposed to have a private citizen by the name of Manual Estevez, mint one centavo coins up to 15,000 pesos and three centavo coins up to 10,000 pesos in 1889. This proposal, after much debate, died in the legislative branch. However, unlike other administrations, though, the Menendez administration decided to use its executive powers and went ahead to place an order with an established mint. The administration decided to hire the Birmingham mint in England to produce both one centavo and three centavo coins. The propose amounts of coins for both one centavo and three centavo coins were exactly the same ones the Estevez contract had called for.

Although, the monetary laws of 1883 set the content and designs for all future manufacturing coins, the Birmingham issues and future ones would deviate from the law. No one knows why the government decided to deviate from the monetary laws, but a great deal of coins would still follow the monetary law of 1883.

Sample: The Birmingham series of 1 and 3 centavos

A temporary tax on coffee led to protest and political chaos for President Menendez. This led to a coup by General Carlos Ezeta on June 22, 1890 shortly after taking power he would start a war with conservative minded Guatemala.

General Ezeta came from the small coffee elite group and his government would be the first that would try to abolish whatever policies the coffee elite felt threatened their way of life. By removing the temporary tax on coffee, the government was again under intense economic pressure to find new sources of income. The sudden drop of silver and the spike of gold meant that the government, who mostly relied on silver payment internally, had to pay her debts in gold, thus causing a financial imbalance and leading to a financial crisis.

The problem with taxation and the gold standard

The government, during various months, changed policies on whether to allow exports of silver coins or to add tax on silver exports in order to stop any shortages of the precious metal. The Ezeta government did commission groups; composed of businesses, to study the impact of banning silver from being exported via tariffs through various meetings. Moving to a gold standard was a proposition the commission had proposed. The government decided to propose the gold standard, like many nations at the time and to stop taxing silver exports. On October 21, 1892, the government agreed to establish the gold standard as the nation's monetary policy.

By 1894, the government of General Ezeta had inherited a large deficit and had been struggling to come up with alternative forms of income. The government had seen several years of political struggle when it chose to adopt the gold standard. The reason being was the fact that many people objected to this policy and shortages of coins made enforcing many laws difficult. So, the government decided to go back on its promise and started to tax goods and services. The tax was supposed to aid in filling the government's coffers and in paying down the national debt.

Unfortunately, the decreased price of silver in the marketplace caused the government of Ezeta to increase taxes on the people. This proved to be a monumental mistake by the Ezeta administration, since it caused a popular revolt among the nation's elite. On April 30, 1894, massive revolts took placed that forced the government's hand. A small group of coffee field owners known as the "44" created vast riots throughout the nation. The government of Ezeta could not hold on to power and the government resistance fell once it saw that the riots were too large to control. The coffee growers elected to have General Rafael Gutierrez take over as president of the provincial government until elections could he held. General Rafael Gutierrez won the general elections and became the new president in 1894.

Under General Rafael Gutierrez, the economy would continue on its slow recovery track. The new government quickly rescinded the various taxes on various goods that the Ezeta government had enacted in order to build capital for the national debt. The new administration bowed to seek new sources of income outside of taxation. President Gutierrez was a big supporter of a new plan to try to rekindle and rebuild the old Central American Federation and he would sponsor several meetings with like-minded heads of states in the region to seek a consensus for unification. The meetings held for unification didn't go beyond just talk.

The economy that had haunted previous administrations would come back to haunt the anti-tax administration of President Gutierrez .International prices on coffee collapsed forcing the administration to impose similar unpopular taxes and to tighten budgetary expenses. The market collapse and large deficits would lead to a coup by General Tomas Regalado in 1895.

CHAPTER 5 LA CASA DE MONEDA: THE CENTRAL AMERICAN MINT LIMITED 1892-1896

The Central American Mint Limited

Throughout this chaotic economic and political period, the dream of finally establishing a mint would finally be realized. Various presidents had dreamed of establishing a mint whether it was privatized or owned by the government; the goal was to have control of the national currency. Politics and back room deals were usually the reasons why so many attempts had been made and all of them had failed. Not until 1891 would the government seriously consider the idea of opening a mint, when the legislators decided to grant a French manufacturer, Sindicat General de Monnais de Paris the opportunity to establish a mint within a year.

No one is 100% sure why the Sindicate decided to transfer its rights to the British Central American Mint Limited in 1891, but the Salvadorian government had no objections over the transfer.

Origins

The story of the Central American Mint LTD has been open to speculation. There are very few sources that go into any detail about the establishment of the Central American Mint LTD, in fact most sources only mention the mint when talking about the coins minted between 1892 and 1896. The reasons why the mint was established or the motivations to establish this mint are unknown. What is known is that the directors of the mint, soon after meeting with Salvadorian representatives decided to seek a corporate status from the British government in order to exclusively mint coins for the state of El Salvador. As to how these British investors came to know that this small Central American country needed a mint and that the French firm was willing to sell their exclusive contract is unknown.

The only possible explanation could be that the French firm saw a financial disadvantage to establishing a mint and therefore decided to sell their interest to the Central American Mint LTD. The amount of money, if any, and the transfer of title, unfortunately, has become lost to history.

What is known is that William Elmore and Alfred Stevens decided to incorporate in London in 1891 as the Central American Mint LTD. The founders of the company sold 12,500 shares in the Central American Mint LTD in order to acquire the finances needed to establish and operate a mint in the nation. The 125,000 pounds were divided into 12,500 shares of 10 pounds each and sold to investors in London. Copies of articles of incorporations in the National Archives in London show that the shareholders in the mint were common British citizens, some of whom stated their occupation on the company registry.

The men who bought shares in the Central American Mint LTD were men from various professions, such as: shoemakers, bakers, businessmen, and lawyers. The company was incorporated in London on November 12, 1891 and her sole purpose, according to the statement of intent, was to establish a mint in El Salvador .Furthermore the documents filed with the National Archives state that both Mr. Elmore and Mr. Stevens signed the agreement with the Salvadorian government on April 29, 1891 and agreed to incorporate on November 6, 1891.

The documents filed with the British government clearly spelled out the activities of what the Central American Mint LTD would be doing in El Salvador in order to produce coins, such as purchasing land or renting equipment. As far as paperwork is concerned, for the period when the mint was active in El Salvador between 1892 and 1896, no other legal paperwork can be found at the British National Archives outside of the company's initial statement.

By mid-1892, the mint had several coins in pre-production, but wanted the government to amend the strict 1883 guidelines on what denominations and what sizes to mint. The Ezeta government agreed and loosened the strict monetary laws for the mint.

On Sunday August 28, 1892 the president of the republic Carlos Ezeta inaugurated the nation's first mint or Casa de Moneda. Although, the government officially declared the mint open on September 3, 1892, the nation's first coins were produced later in the afternoon of August 28, 1892 after the presidents inaugural speech.

From Peso to Colon

The creation of a national mint partially solved the lack of currency in the country, but added political instability between the mint and the government. The original contract called for the mint to produce several silver and gold coins for a 20 year span, but soon after the first manufactured coins, the government decided to breach her contract.

The first problem the mint would experience occurred with the sudden change in the legislative decision to change the national currency to honor the 400th anniversary of Christopher Columbus. On October 1 1892 the legislation decided to call all silver pesos "Colon" as an honor to Columbus. Henceforth, the national currency of El Salvador would become known as the Colon.

The legislation called for the 50 centavos and one peso silver coins to be called Colones as well. The design featuring the bust of Columbus and his name surrounded by Un Colon and America Central on the bottom. The back features the national seal.

The problem the mint encountered with the switch from Peso to Colon for the silver one peso was that the mint had already manufactured coins of 50 centavo and one peso denominations. These coins featured the national flag wrapped on a pole on the face value and the "America Central" around the flag. The back featured the national emblem and Republica Del Salvador spelled out. These coins would quickly disappear from circulation and replaced with the Columbus coin.

Sample :1892 Colon Coin

The first Columbus colon has a date of 1892 even though they were manufactured in early 1893. This was a decision taken by the mint. The majority of the previous flag 50 centavo and one peso coins were melted to use in future Columbus one colon coins. As a result, all one and 50 centavo flag coins would become rare.

The second problem for the Central American Mint LTD was that it manufactured coins that were not approved or negotiated by the government. For example, the one centavo cooper coin was a coin of necessity that was greatly needed in a market that lacked small denominations. Yet, the one centavo coin was not approved by the government and therefore most were melted. Thus, the 1 centavo coin had joined the flag 50 centavo and one peso coins in scarcity in the numismatic history of the country. The one centavo coin was made out of copper with a cap featured on its face value and a back featuring a one centavo surrounded by an olive branch and the wording "Central America".

Between 1892 and early 1893 the government went out of its way to reassure the public that the silver and gold contents were of specific precious metal content. The government sent samples of the coins minted in the Central American Mint LTD to a private American company, Seaby Smelting and Lead Company and to the U.S mint. Once the coins had been examined and the reports forwarded to the government, they were immediately published so all citizens could feel confident that the coins being manufactured were of the appropriate silver and gold content.

Another coin minted that was not supposed to have been was the 2 ½ peso gold coin. Based on the legislative decree of October 21 1892 that placed the country on the gold standard, the gold coins that were supposed to be minted were the: five, ten, and twenty gold peso gold coins. Unlike the previous coins that were recalled and melted, the 2 ½ peso coin survived due to the fact that the nation was experiencing a shortage of small denominations of gold coin.

The financial crisis the nation was experiencing made the government re-think her fiscal and monetary policies. During 1893, the nation had experienced a shift from a silver monetary policy to that of a gold monetary policy that would alter how the nation would conduct business. The same year, the actions and unpopular policies of President Ezeta led to a coup by General Gutierrez. The new government was very conservative and one of the first actions taken by the legislation was to review the contract between the mint and the state. Unfortunately, for the Central American Mint LTD, the new administration revised the previous agreement.

Shortly after the government decided to void the agreement by canceling the contract between the Ezeta government and the Central American Mint LTD, it caused the mint to stop production in February 1893. Shortly afterwards talks resumed until a new contract was reached between the parties.

The new agreement between the government and the Central American Mint LTDwas made on July 6, 1893. The agreement called for the following:

    A. A new lease for five years in order to complete the government order

B. The re-minting of all silver coins and minting of national coins to the total value of 5 million pesos

C. The mint would be paid $12 pesos for every $100 pesos minted

D. At the end of the five years, the government would recover the original proofs

Furthermore, the mint had the responsibility of seeking out and acquiring the coins to be melted or re-minting by the nation's banks. The mint re-started operations on July 19, 1893.

Shortly, after the new agreement, the mint would run into problems when it came to acquiring the silver to produce coins. The shortage of coins led to a public announcement by the mint to purchase old silver coins from the public. The government quickly banned the exportation of silver coins.

The missing 25 centavo coin

Wages in the country were mostly paid through: old real coins, tokens or foreign currency circulating in the country. In the farming estates, tokens were the most common mean of payment to workers in the fields. Most salaries, outside the estates, were paid in small currency, especially the twenty and four centavo coins, therefore after hearing complains and doing research the government decided to mint a twenty five centavo coin that would help pay wages. The propose coin by the Central American Mint Limited looked exactly like the twenty centavo coin that was in circulation and had been minted. Unfortunately, the mint and the government never came to terms on an agreement to mint these coins.

The uneasy relationship between the government and the Central American Mint Limited ended on January 1896 when the mint announced it had re-minted the five million silver coins it had renegotiated with the government in 1893.

The relationship between the mint and the state after 1893 had progressively worsened due to the unstable government contracts and lack of raw material to mint coins. After it had concluded her contract the mint would continue to have difficulties with the state over payment. First, the mint was ordered by the government to return to the treasury the models used to produce the coins. Secondly, the government took an inventory check of the machinery used by the mint in the thought that they might acquire the machinery for future production. Sadly, the government decided to abandon this idea as well. Third, the mint wanted to give the government a few thousand one centavo pieces as part of the ongoing negotiations over an agreement.

However, just like the previous one centavo offers to the government, the government refused to accept them correctly advising the mint that it was never part of any contract and that the matter should have been settled years earlier in a separate negotiation. Finally, the mint felt cheated enough that it filed grievances with the government claiming it had lost money because of the shortages of silver. The mint argued that thanks to the protective clauses, the government had instituted, it had led to the mint losing money by delaying production and by acquiring raw materials at a higher cost.

Was the CAM worth it?

The agreement between the government and the Central American Mint LTD has been portrayed by many numismatic experts as a deal that was too expensive. Much of the theory behind the cost of minting coins in the country comes from Dr. Jacinto Castellanos the Minister of Foreign Relations who heavily criticized the previous Ezeta administration's handling of the contract as too expensive. Dr. Castellanos, argued in his report to the congress in 1896, that minting coins in England or importing them would have been cheaper than both the initial and modified contract the governments had agreed to with the mint.

Many attribute these comments by a high ranking minister to show that indeed the country had spent too much money on a private mint. However, Dr. Castellanos never gave estimates of how much the nation would have saved if the country had decided to continue to export their coin production. We cannot compare production cost for El Salvador with other Central American countries that already had mints at the time and whose financial resources and raw materials were different. Some authors have used this method to conclude that Dr. Castellanos argument was correct. In my opinion, this argument is not foolproof and we can only speculate as to whether any agreement was indeed a financial loss to the government.

Whatever the case, the decision by the government was to place on hold any ideas to establish a mint. The former building that held the Central American Mint LTD was converted to the national press office.

As the many events show, the ending of the Casa de Moneda was considered by the government to be a great achievement, since many had argued that it had cost the nation too much money in the first place to establish a mint. This can explain why the Ezeta government held such hostility toward the mint for it saw it as one of the biggest unnecessary expenditures the nation had undertaken. The cancelation by the Ezeta government and renegotiation of the mint contract might have saved the nation money, but in the end many felt they still overpaid.

After the Central American Mint LTD closed shop in 1896, the government had the option of either establishing its own mint with the dies it had acquired from the mint or partnering up with another private firm to operate the national mint. Unfortunately, due to economic problems and political instability the government failed to establish another mint.

The Liquidation of the Central American Mint Limited

By 1896, the mint had completed the last number of coins the revised 1893 contract had stated and the Central American Mint LTD was relieved of duty in the country. The Central American Mint LTD did not operate any other mint nor did it choose to invest in other projects after its closing in 1896. Instead, the shareholders of the company decided to voluntarily dissolve the company on July 17, 1899. A special resolution was adopted by the shareholders and the two people appointed to liquidate the company were the two founders Spencer Barclay Heward and John Jepson Atkinson. Liquidation of the company's assets and liabilities was completed by November 1899.

For the next two decades, the government of El Salvador would still use the CAM mint mark on its one colon coins. These one colon coins were manufactured in both American mint facilities and in other foreign countries. After 1914, the CAM mint would disappear from all currency and the country would choose several new designs.

The government of El Salvador would never re-establish another mint, instead it would rely on foreign governments and private mints to manufacture her currency.

The Era of Protective Decrees

The federal government fearing that without new coins in circulation a silver shortage would be probable, decided in 1896 to ban the exportation of silver. The closure of the Central American Mint LTD caused the government to come up with a law to protect the silver coins that were minted during the previous years. The new decree prohibited anyone from exporting domestic and international silver located in the country; in essence all silver coins in circulation. This law lasted just one year before being repealed.

By 1899 the government decided to institute a new decree that would be more efficient and more enforceable. On March 7, 1899 the government issued a new decree that would make silver exportation more manageable. The new law would established a levy of 30% upon all coined silver exported. Also, the new law rewarded citizens by paying up to a 2% premium on all silver coins imported into the country.

Months after the March decree, the government, decided on May 5, 1899 to repeal the previous decrees due to the difficulty of enforcing the laws. The government though, kept a law on the books that prohibited importing silver coins with less than 0.900 silver content.

Conclusion

The 19th century was a chaotic century for El Salvador. The 19th century saw the state gain independence as part of the Central American Federation and become an independent nation. However, the state would suffer decades of economic and political turmoil. Throughout the century, the nation would lack a national coin due to the lack of resources to either establish a mint or to have them manufactured by a country. Instead, the government would rely on coins from various nations and in the few coins manufactured from the federation period as currency. By the end of the century, the first national coins were ordered and the nation's first mint was established. By the start of the 20th century, the nation would be stable enough too finally decommission foreign currency and tokens and rely solely on its own national currency.

CHAPTER 6
A NEW MILLENNIUM: THE ARISTOCRATIC PRESIDENCIES 1900-1932

Overview of the first half of the century 1900-1932

Politically speaking the start of the 20th century was much more stable than the previous century. The start of the decade would continue to see presidential administrations that were not interested in investing in the infrastructure of the country. The need for schools and medical facilities was not a priority. However, providing a friendly environment for coffee planters that included little to no taxes and no government regulation was the standard policy of all administrations of the era. Frankly, the presidents that ran the country from the late 1880s to 1913 were forgettable.

However, politics in the country would change with the 1913 elections that saw Carlos Melendez win the presidency. Melendez was one of the nation's elite and with his election he set the stage for what eventually would become a hostile political environment that would lead to the nation's military coup in 1932. Melendez would create a political dynasty in the country that would dominate the presidency for the next two decades. The president was so powerful that he named his successor not from the political party apparatus, but from branches of his own family.

The growth of the public sector unions and independent trade unions grew in the early years of the Carlos Melendez administration and with that debt also grew. Unfortunately, for all the plans the administration had sought, the outbreak of the First World War, limited the amount of demand for coffee and thus exports fell causing revenue for the state to decline. However, the Melendez administration didn't cut down on expenses and instead would continue investing and expanding the economy by investing in new projects such as roads and railroad tracks. Even though the benefits for modernizing the country were good, the people who most benefited from his projects were the coffee exporters and the agricultural industry. These businessmen now had modern roads and faster railways to get their products to ports in a cheaper and faster way than ever before.

The Belgium of Central America

For the first 30 years of the 20th century, the political atmosphere in El Salvador seemed to reflect a new era for the country. The new century saw the coffee export grow that made a few investors wealthy. It was a booming time for artist and writers, writers like Alberto Masferrer, who had the freedom to write and speak their mind. Trade unions and even left leaning unions were founded without opposition from those in power.

However, no official political party could challenge the National Democratic Party or its patriarch President Quinonez. However, putting politics aside, the country was prospering in the arts and for a period of time becoming financially better off than her neighbors.

Many writers felt that the country was aligning and following the Costa Rican model. Some bankers even spoke of the fact that El Salvador would surpass Costa Rica and become a prosperous small nation like Belgium.

However, the civilian presidents failed to modernize or diversify the economy. By the time of the Great Depression the collapse of commodity prices would devastate coffee prices and send the economy of El Salvador into a downfall. Worse, it created an atmosphere of fear and intimidation that would conclude with General Hernandez coup of 1932. Whatever gains were made during the last three decades they were lost under an atmosphere of fear of reform which many elite conveniently called communism. Time ran out for reform by 1932. It would take several decades and a civil war for a democratically elected president to be elected again.

The grains of gold

Coffee had played an important part in the late 19th century land reform that saw millions of acres of land being taken over by the government and wealthy farmers at the expense of the native population. The country didn't have many banks to lend money and no real currency to circulate among the population outside of countermarked coins from previous decades and from foreign countries. With the start of the Banco Salvadoreno in the late 19th century, the bank started to mint paper money. However revolutionary the idea of having a bank was to citizens, the bank quickly became a symbol of the elitist institutions running the country.

Unlike today in our modern economies, banks in the late 19th and early 20th century, worldwide only catered to big businesses and government institutions. Banco Salvadoreno really became a default central bank for the government when it was authorized to print paper money and later in 1904 when a constitutional amendment allowed banks to order coins. Throughout the late 19th century and early 20th century, Banco Salvadoreno became the biggest and most influential bank in the country.

After several years of shortages of national coins, the government finally decided to pass legislation allowing banks to mint coins on the states behalf. The law went into effect on May 5, 1904 and allowed the banks to:

-
-

a. Furnish national dies in order for silver coins to be minted abroad

b. All national coins were to be order through a national bank and be in accordance to federal law.

c. Banks were responsible for coins to meet the standards.

Under the law, the government would authorize the production of the 1904 peso silver coins. Under this law, productions of coins would continue for decades.

The 1904-1910 1 Colon Series

The new colon coins were of the exact design of the ones produced by the Central American Mint LTD (CAM). However, these coins were minted by the United States mint. These coins were minted at the San Francisco mint and the Nevada mint.

Although these coins were minted in the United States, they still showed the mint mark of the CAM and had no mint marks for either the San Francisco or Nevada mints. Apparently, the Salvadorian government didn't want to change the design of the coin.

The business of lending money to farmers was normally handled through private businessmen and large farming institutions before and after the establishment of Banco Salvadoreno. Like most banks of the time, Banco Salvadoreno lent money to the most influential families with long term loans and average interest. However, the small farmers and middle class workers didn't have the capital requirements to obtain loans.

If you were a small farmer with a few acres of land dedicated to coffee or dye your best bet of getting a short term loan was to visit the wealthy landowner in the region or to take up a loan from an investor. However, these loans were not only risky, but potentially detrimental to the borrower. The reason was that a farmer had to put up his property as collateral and even set up a portion of the product as payment just in case the loan couldn't be paid back. Frankly, it was similar to how a pawn shop operates .Instead of leaving an item to pawn, you just sign over the deed to your property and/or future gains on coffee grains.

Needless to say, that although the country's dependence on coffee increased it wasn't the working class or small middle class that benefited, but the old families and new bankers who quickly benefited from increased coffee prices and cheap lands lost by defaulters of loans.

It was evident that the status quo couldn't continue in a country that was becoming more dependent on a single crop. Many intellectuals started to openly question the lack of government interference in the private sector for fear that the inequalities would increase the poverty rate of the nation. In order to make the economy more diverse however, the state needed to start instigating new foreign investments and to start encouraging new banks to open in order for these institutions to lend to the common citizen.

Pure Laissez Faire

It's difficult to imagine a country that had no checks and balances when it came to running the economy. However small, El Salvador was by the turn of the 20th century, a laissez faire economy with almost no government interference. The fact that the government had no central bank clearly shows that the country was dependant on a free open market for her goods and to determine her monetary policies.

However, El Salvador clearly is an example of a country that depended almost exclusively on one agricultural product: coffee. When the commodity prices increased the elite and the workers benefited. However, when the commodity prices for coffee fell, the workers usually were either laid off or not paid. The reason why workers are an important part of the economy of El Salvador in this era was because most were seasonal workers whose labor was needed in order to harvest and plant the coffee in the fields. When workers couldn't work it meant more unemployment and poverty. This seasonal occurrence was a minor inconvenience to those in power. However, having large amount of masses demanding pay and work had all the ingredients for an uprising that was evident to come sooner or later. In essence, keeping a strong fiscal policy was evident to all the presidents. Otherwise a potential coup was clearly in play if no recovery could be made. This is the reason why during the time of the Central American Mint LTD the country's political class was in chaos seeing several generals leading coups to obtain power.

The Gold Standard

The gold standard monetary policy had become a failure for the country back went it was implemented in the late 1890's. Yet economic factors caused the government to once again implement and adopt the gold standard in the early 20th century.

The start of the First World War caused many ripple effects throughout the world. In the case of El Salvador it would be a lack of silver to cover the peso. When the war started, merchants demanded payment for credit outstanding and silver became a precious commodity.

With no federal reserve bank, the country couldn't do much to control her currency when a growing number of citizens started to redeem their paper money and their coinsfor silver. Therefore, the government announced a moratorium in the redemption of silver until a year after the end of the war. Thus, the government could hold on to her silver reserves to cover her needs.

Ironically, the silver crises led to an unexpected windfall for the government after the end of the great war saw a spike in demand for silver. By 1920, the price of silver was high enough that the government decided that it served their interest to liquidate her silver bullion holdings. By selling the silver at the time the country gained a windfall in profits. The move to liquidate silver caused the country to adopt the gold standard for a second time on September 11, 1919.

Following the decision to adopt the gold standard, the nation passed a new decree demonetizing all domestic and international silver coins in circulation with the exception of the following silver coins: five, ten, and twenty centavo coins.

The Quinonez Administration 1913-1922

Alfonso Quinonez was the most powerful politician in the National Democratic Party during the early 20th century. Quinonez would obtain the presidency on three occasions: 1914, 1918 and 1923. The decision not to run for a consecutive second term was a constitutional one. Instead Quinonez would have a party loyalist fill the presidency until he could officially run for office.

Nevertheless, President Quinonez wanted to expand his political base to ensure no opposition to his rule. Therefore he courted both the public employees unions and their rivals the trade unions.

In order to keep an eye out for dissent he instituted a new paramilitary force to help him keep an eye on any opposition. This was the environment in which the National Guard was created back in the early 1900s'. Although he had a monopoly on the presidency and a new police agency to help him keep power he went ahead and instituted martial law. Thus, guaranteeing no opposition during his many presidential terms.

The mortgage crisis continued

The fact that farmers were losing their properties when they couldn't repay loans and that those properties were either ending up in the hands of the big landowners or in the hands of wealthy immigrants made the dream of land ownership a theory. Many scholars proposed creating a central bank to finance loans for farmers, but there was never a strong political will to do so.

President Quinonez in 1919 decided to propose a "banco de riqueza nacional" (national wealth bank), that would loan money on fair terms to farmers. He wanted to create a re-payment structure that would allow the farmers to repay the bank without the risk of them losing their lands.

However, nothing came out of this proposed idea, so Mr. Abraham Rivera, a coffee planter and leader of a small group of farmers, proposed a different bank structure. Under Rivera's plan, the bank would lend out money to all farmers, but at a rate of 6%. The payments the bank would obtain would then be re-invested in Salvadorian bonds, thus guaranteeing that the money would be invested in the nation.

A study was published in 1921 by a well known Salvadorian banker named Berlamino Sanchez. He urged politicians to create a financial reform package to solve the crisis. Otherwise, he predicted, the country would need 15 years of direct investments from a central bank or he warned in a manner of decades the country would literally be in the hands of a few elite families owning most of the lands. Suarez pointed out that banks would lend money for a period of nine months at interest rates that were as high as 18%. Sanchez wanted and urged a sensible solution to this major economic problem.

After World War 1, the price of coffee sky rocketed to $20 in 1919, but quickly fell for the next two years to $11 and $12. The laissez faire policies were making small farmers lose their lands at an alarming rate. Yet, the Quinonez administration was unable to push for changes in the legislative branch. The same banking policies would remain in place for another decade.

Plans to Mint

The most serious attempt at re-establishing a mint was discussed in 1920. The law dated July 15, 1920 set an ambitious plan for the minting of several new gold coins and new non-silver denominations. The revenue of the sale of gold made the government over enthusiastic about the idea of minting new coins. The gold coins that were proposed were the: five, ten, twenty and forty gold colon coin. Also, new non- silver coins of: three, twenty, fifty and one hundred centavo coins were proposed.

Unfortunately, none of the gold coins were ever minted due to the unforeseen Wall Street crash that hampered any attempts to mint gold coins. As for the other coins, most would be eventually minted over the course of the next decades by the U.S mint.

Coins Shortages and Eventual Demonization of Silver

The demonization of silver coins caused a shortage of coins that led to citizens demanding the government to allow them to continue to use their silver. Popular protest, in February 1921, caused the government to reconsider the decree that banned all silver coins from circulation. After much thought, it was decided to allow citizens, temporarily, to continue using silver coins until further notice or until it was determined that there was a sufficient amount of non silver coins in the market.

Unlike in the past century, the government was committed to issuing her own currency through paper money and non precious metals for her coins. The demonizing of all silver coins by the state and the commitment to authorize the manufacture of coins to replace them made a ban more successfully implemented. The state chose non-precious metals such as copper nickel to replace her vast silver holdings. By 1934 the state decided to establish a central bank that would govern all currency circulating in the country.

Slowly heading toward disaster

The alarming rate that farmers were losing their lands, was cause for concern, however, the federal government had an even bigger concern. Apparently, the nation had accumulated a huge deficit. Why? It seemed that President Quinonez and his colleagues had invested large sums of money on improving the nation's capital infrastructure and in giving "gifts" to their union supporters. Furthermore, the president had hired thousands of unneeded union workers. These political tactics gained the president thousands of votes. However, by the 1920's El Salvador had more public employees on payroll than any other state in Central America.

Another fiscal headache for the state was the army. President Quinonez and his colleagues wanted to professionalize the armed forces. This goal, although noble, came at a high price. The country had not fought a war with a sister state in decades and the power of the old conservative Guatemalan landowners was all but gone. Yet, the various governments of the era felt a need to maintain a large army. Clearly, the army had gained much during the many presidencies of Quinonez.

Overall, the federal government needed to maintain her clout by using the civil service branch and the armed forces as political bases to keep the Quinonez-Menendez dynasty in power. However, the government also felt a need to support local capital residents by subsidizing between 17-30% of all capital employees involved in small trade unions. As a result, the deficit increased and the lack of a diverse economy would ultimately lead to major political pressure for the future leaders of the country.

The Mortgage crisis impacts the economy

By the mid 1920's, the country had several crises it needed to address. All were either related or caused by the lack of credit given to small farmers. When the farmers lost their lands in effect it usually ended up in the hands of the coffee elite who in turn converted those lands to coffee fields. However, although coffee was abundant many "butterfly effect" changes occurred all across the country.

The continued foreclosures of lands of small and middle class farmers led to a migration of citizens to Honduras , where land was plentiful and loans were fairer. Several thousand Salvadorians immigrated to Honduras and many would not return for several decades. Ironically, the future political problems between Honduras and El Salvador would be traced back to this era of massive immigrant departures.

Those farmers who didn't migrate chose to go to the capital to seek work. This led to an increased dense population in San Salvador which led to many social ills ranging from a rise of alcoholism to a rise in crime. The capital city had no resources to deal with an abundance of migrant workers.

The trade unions that once held a strong political base and that could have in the past employed these farmers was now struggling to be relevant in a new political environment. The large unions had all but replaced the political base of the trade unions who were now struggling to survive. This led to even more people being left unemployed.

Finally, the cost of food increased several percentage points. This was due, ironically, to the fact that many fields were being used only for the production of coffee. Those farmers that had lost lands had in fact not only farmed coffee beans, but also food. When those farmers lost their lands it led to reduction of food being grown. Thus, food was either exported or was being sold at premium prices at the markets. Those who couldn't afford the increased prices were left facing starvation.

Who was to be blame for the lack of action? Journalists like Alberto Masferrer blamed the political elite for not having the backbone to diversify the economy. Others blame the traditional coffee elite that were reluctant to embrace new economic policies because of the fear that it would endanger their businesses. In fact, the traditional coffee elite instead of embracing the many proposals for a central bank chose to establish the Associacion Cafetelera a special interest group whose sole purpose was to finance its holdings.

Finally, the growing number of wealthy foreigners obtaining foreclose lands and setting up shop in the country created a backlash against immigrants. Much like any country going through a difficult economic period immigrants became the scapegoats that politicians and elite families would bash . Honestly, all these sectors in the Salvadorian economy were to be blamed for creating such a crisis that worsened once the Great Depression sank the commodity prices of coffee beans.

A Glimpse of Hope

The election of President Pio Romero Bosque in 1927 didn't create much excitement. Many experts believed that this lawyer and nephew of Quinonez was just another puppet of the former president. However, President Bosque would dramatically change the political landscape of the land by exiling Quinonez.

The expulsion of former President Quinonez by President elect Bosque was hailed as the biggest political coup of the era. He chose to expel the man that had not only dominated the presidency in the last two decades, but that had chosen him, a member of the family as his successor. This action, ironically, brought the new president a great deal of support from not only rivals of the former president but also from Quinonez's past allies who had grown tired of seeing Quinonez run the country for so long. Another executive order by Bosque lifted the martial law that his predecessors had kept in order to control political dissent. President Bosque was not afraid of his rivals nor was he afraid of the people, his administration would lay the groundwork for a transition to free democratic elections.

President Bosque acquired a country that was on the verge of economic disaster. The previous administrations had decided to keep the country from defaulting on her debt, by cutting down the deficit and by subsiding fewer trade unions. The previous administration had acquire a loan from a New York bank and was obligated to keep an American banker in the port. By 1931, the government was spending a third of her income or 6,000,000 colones out of 15,000,000 colones coming in every year paying down the debt.

During his term, the deficit would drop, yet the prices of coffee and cost of basic goods were still under no control. El Salvador's exports were now going to European powers and the United States combined exports and imports from El Salvador dropped during the 20's. Efforts were also made to invest locally and not internationally in order to build the infrastructure of the country. All in all, President Bosque tried to get a handle on the economy, but felt that the country needed true leadership to lead it through hard times.

The Self-Sustain Elites

In terms of whether the country's economic problems were a result of a laizze faire environment or corruption, the answer is simple it was laizze faire. The country's elite whether they had been coffee owners or generals all were well taken care of by the state or by the private sector. Frankly, the curse of an overbearing bureaucracy didn't exist since the state didn't regulate much. In terms of financing, the elite didn't bother getting loans from the government or getting political favors since many politicians were wealthy elite coffee planters. If anything, the political environment was set to turn away any economic reform that would slow down business in the country's three major banks that were controlled by a few families.

When it came to banking the elite would go to one of three banking institutions in the country. The largest and oldest was Banco de Occidente controlled by the Bloom family. For a period of time the bank enjoyed a monopoly in the industry and up to the first quarter of the 20th century was the biggest investment vehicle in the country.

However, competition from Banco Salvadoreno and Banco Agricola Commercial made the playing field more competitive. One thing was sure; the elite didn't have much trouble obtaining credit from banks.

The decision

President Bosque by 1931 decided to make a major announcement. The President decided to allow for the first time free presidential elections. This was an unprecedented announcement, since few expected that the presidency could be up for election. However, Bosque felt that the decrease deficit and progressive years in the last couple of decades had improved the country's social base enough that holding free elections was the next step in creating future prosperity.

Bosque went a step further by not naming a successor or supporting a particular party. That meant that groups ranging from communist to fascist could register their party and candidate to run for office. Thankfully, neither one of these extremists got much support and the moderate parties ran their top candidates in the general election. Concern was blooming when two generals Maximiliano Hernandez Martinez and Claramont ran under two different political parties, since many believed the army was vying for the top political job in the land. However, President Bosque reassured the citizens that although they were army generals they were running as civilians and didn't represent the will of the armed forces.

By 1931, an unlikely candidate rose in the labor party in Arturo Araujo. Araujo a British educated trained engineer wanted a moderate approach to government and his party appealed to several politically minded citizens. However, a myth was brewing when word was spreading among his supporters that Araujo would radically redistribute land in the first couple of days of his administration. Regardless of the many rumors, Araujo found so much support that even rivals like Gen. Maximilano Hernandez supported Araujo's candidacy.

The Rise and Fall of Araujo's Government

Arturo Araujo, the labor party's candidate won the presidency on December 2 1931. When President Araujo won the election he wanted to solve the country's problems by not alienating the elite, but by forming a consensus cabinet. The United States government was more than happy to support Araujo and his consensus policies hoping that he would democratically change the country's economic problems. Unfortunately, Araujo's presidency would last only nine months due to a series of blunders committed by his administration ranging from corrupt administrators to having a powerful general as vice president. The coup that installed Gen Martinez ended the hopes of a democratic movement for more than 50 years.

The problem was that the majority of career bureaucrats were either too loyal to the opposition or didn't want any part of the labor party. Thus, Araujo had to nominate party loyalist who were both political appointees with no experience and people that unfortunately became corrupt. The administrations incompetence would become one of three factors that would lead to Arajo's downfall.

The second mistake Araujo made was to appoint as vice president Gen. Maximiliano Hernandez Martinez. The general did not resign from the armed forces to become a civilian vice president, instead he appointed himself as the minister of defense. By having two prominent administrative roles, Hernandez was in a perfect position to manage all security forces. By making Hernandez the second most powerful man in government, the president made the armed forces the most political institution in the country.

It's true that there was no way President Araujo would know that Gen Martinez would one day betray him. However, there were too many red flags to show that Martinez was obtaining too much power. For example, by becoming the secretary of war he personally placed allied colonels and generals in positions of influence in the new administration. Thus, Gen Hernandez was seen by many to be the power broker in the Araujo government.

There is no concrete evidence to suggest that Hernandez orchestrated the coup that some believe he was indeed lucky to be in the right place at the right time to take advantage of the situation.

The truth is somewhere in the middle, but Araujo appointed a man whom he felt could unite the army behind him and keep an eye on the opposition. He even married his daughter to Martinez, so that he could have family ties to Araujo. In the end, the chance to obtain power was too good to resist for Martinez.

The last and biggest mistake committed by President Araujo was in not clarifying his political message regarding land reform during his campaign. It's true that Araujo never promised land reform, knowing that this would be a major contention with the coffee elite, but his supporters unfortunately came to believe this rumor. During the 1920's, coffee represented 90% of all exports and the country was the only one in Central America to depend on only one crop for most of its revenue. Thus, any land reform proposal, in this era, would have been contentious and most likely full of compromises with the elite.

Many far left supporters went out of their way to support Araujo and in trying to get support from the large native Indian population they made claims that Araujo could never fulfill. Once Araujo took power, these peasants staged protest and events to push the government to keep the land reform promise that they had heard so much about. Araujo's government failed to cool heads and the growing uncertainty by the coffee elite led the military to publicly demand a crack down on what they perceived were agitators.

In the end Araujo misread both his base and the security forces, since he couldn't appease either group. Sadly, in his nine months in office, President Araujo was a lame duck president failing to address either his supporters or his rivals and in essence created a political vacuum that led to the army leading a coup to overthrow him.

CHAPTER 7 THE END OF A DREAM: THE DICTATORSHIP OF GENERAL MARTINEZ 1932-1944

The Coup and the massacre

It might have been a surprise to President Araujo, but everyone saw a potential coup brewing in the army, yet Araujo was ignorant of one led by so many army officers. The stock market crash had all but destroyed the export coffee business and many more were left homeless or in debt. Worse, migrant workers were out of work and those that could find work were paid pennies.

In his book 1932, author Thomas Anderson recounts an example of what a migrant farm worker got paid and how much a plantation owner would make of his coffee harvest. He points out that a man could earn as much as 12 cents per day and get a meal that would cost one penny. The owners of the plantation spent around $12,000 pounds in labor and feeding cost on workers, but they earned over $100,000 pounds on coffee. The average wages for workers ranged from 50 cents per day to 20 or lower, however the great depression made wages on the lower end the norm.

The huge discrepancies made life a lot harder for the working poor and in 1931, the growing number of unemployed started to openly resent their bosses.

Whether it was the inability of the government to pay their wages or the unfair banking reform policies presented by the president, the army by the summer of 1931 was already planning a coup. On the night of December 2, 1931, the army finally staged the coup after news broke of their plot being discovered.

Although the armed forces were determined to stage a coup, it ran into resistance from security forces and army barracks that remained loyal to President Araujo. After a couple of days of fighting, the armed forces took control of the government, but feared rebel peasants in the rural areas of the country.

Meanwhile, vice president General Maximilian Hernandez Martinez was placed with the consent of the US Consulate as provincial president. Martinez had agreed to hold free elections as soon as his provincial presidency period expired. Why was Martinez placed in power? Did he plan the whole coup? Answers to these questions are debatable. However, scholars agreed that the army could not place an outsider as provincial president, because the 1923 Latin America accord forbade the United States government from recognizing a military coup. Thus, General Martinez took over and quickly squashed resistance.

President Araujo fled to Guatemala where he found an ally in the Guatemalan president. Araujo promised his supporters that he would return. Martinez, fearing an invasion, decided to clamp down on dissent and to rule under a state of emergency, meaning no elections would be held. In a matter of months, Gen. Martinez went from eing an unknown general running for office to running the country as a sole dictator.

The US government quickly broke relations with El Salvador over the suspension of elections. However, the general would bond closely with the axis powers during his early reign making Washington rethink her previous diplomatic stand. Eventually, the US government would recognize his administration as democratically elected, but only after some cosmetic changes to his government had been implemented such as sham elections and military run political parties to ensure Martinez's election.

The legacy of General Hernandez is the 1932 massacre. Scholars estimate that over 30,000 people, mostly Indians, were killed. Hernandez feared several possible challenges to his reign ranging from a: possible invasion from Araujo's supported from Guatemala, a communist insurrection or a peasant uprising. Thus, he decided to clamp down hard on the riots that broke out in January 1932. The riots took place over a course of days as many towns saw large amounts of peasants staging protest against their wealthy and oppressive plantation owners. The peasants had come to believe that President Araujo had been deposed, because he was trying to pass land reform and that the president needed their help in order to return to power.

A myth quickly spread among the army that communists were behind the uprisings. An infamous young communist named Farmundo Marti had been the leader of the communist party of El Salvador. He had been arrested and detained in prior years and even ran as president against Araujo. Marti, ever the opportunist, hatched a quick plan to join the peasant revolt. He wired Moscow that the time had come for El Salvador to become a communist state. However, Moscow didn't take him seriously and quickly dismissed the uprising as peasant related and not communist inspired. Yet, Marti took to the streets spreading lies and joining the crowds in protesting. Marti's followers joined some mobs and spread chaos in many rural areas of the country. General Martinez took advantage of the myth of communist infiltration to have his forces kill many poor Indian peasants in the name of order.

The massacre of 1932 all but seal the fate that no democratic elections would be held as long as Martinez was in power. The armed forces for days massacred entire villages in the peasant communities. The peasants were all accused of being communist supporters and were quickly executed by firing squads. There were never any trials or proof that the majority of those being killed had ever rebelled against their bosses. Yet, the army thought it more efficient to kill as many Indians, since many resented their bosses and the risk of another uprising was not something General Hernandez was prepared to endure.

By killing so many innocent civilians the general had sent a message: don't oppose my rule or otherwise you will be accused of communism and be quickly executed.

A Madmen

Some scholars have argued that General Martinez didn't have all his mental faculties. After all, executing so many people could only be an act of a madman. There is some evidence to support the theory that Martinez was indeed mentally unstable.

For example, Martinez was a big advocate of the occult. Although he was not an atheist, he wasn't a religious man either. His personal beliefs were controversial. On one famous occasion the general, after a tarot reading, decided to wrap the entire street lights of the capital in red paper for the night. Naturally, the psychic had warned him that by doing so he was protecting the country from attracting evil spirits.

Although the general didn't have the brightest mind he did succeed in solving the banking dilemma where others had failed. Although, thankfully, the general did not personally establish the Central Bank he had enough foresight to know that the country needed this institution and decided not to politicize the bank.

The Central Bank

The administration of General Hernandez was under intense pressure to resolve the economic problems the country was encountering with credit and currency. In order to bring more stability to the banking system, the administration decided to commission a study that would examine the nation's economic structure. By 1931, there were only four banks in the country and all of them in the hands of or under the influence of the elite families that ran El Salvador.

Under Salvadorian law, banks had the option of ordering coins and paper money for the country. The issuing of coins was at the discretion of the banks in the country. While banks were allowed to order coins for the country, all the designs were of the same standards. However, when it came to paper money, the banks could print whatever amount of bills in whatever designs they wanted. Needless to say that by the Great Depression the country was in great need of a central bank to regulate her currency since there was no guarantee that those banks wouldn't default.

For the banking study, the administration decided to look for a banker outside the country that had the experience of working in the international banking scene. British banker Frederick Francis Joseph Powell was brought in to conduct a formal study of the nation's banking system.

By 1934, Frederick Powell had concluded his study and he had determined that the nation was in grave need of establishing a strong central bank that could regulate banks and have the sole power to issue and regulate currency. The Hernandez administration decided to adopt Powell's recommendations and he proposed a new national law that would allow the country to established a central bank. The legislative branch quickly approved the law (over the concerns of some elite families) and on June 19, 1934 the central bank was established.

The Martinez government negotiated successfully with the Duke family that ran Banco Agricola Commercial. The agreement authorized the government to purchase stock from Banco Agricola bank to finance the new central bank. Frederick Powell was appointed the director of the central bank and he brought in several foreign bankers to teach the local government authorities on how to run a central bank . The government decided that even though, the central bank, was set up as a government entity and by public funding, the bank would be set up legally as a limited public company. The decision to not interfere in the banks policies or to have the bank become an institution of the regime aided foreign investor's decision to invest in the country knowing that the bank was not a tool of the Hernandez administration.

It took the central bank several years before it could start to function completely and by the late 1930's the bank was ready to start to issue recommendations and to receive orders from the government when it came to minting coins or in withdrawing currency from the market.

The bank's first problem was in dealing with a lack of silver in the market and the need for the state to phase out its silver coin holdings. Unlike previous decades, when the state had decided to withdraw currency by having citizens go to local government offices, from now on the central bank would be the entity in charge of recalling currency by government decree.

The Hernandez Years

General Hernandez felt that he needed to create a new state that could regulate commerce and aid the less fortunate . Although, he created many social programs to help the working class his real aim was to gather a political base of support among the poor and among government employees. Thus, the government sponsored Pro-Patria party came into existence around the mid 1930's. The party gathered financial support through forced contributions of government employee wages and money supply by the general.

Pro-Patria became the main political machinery in the country that allowed the general to keep his friends and allies in power. He amended the military code in

1935, thus putting an end to coups by imposing major penalties on anyone attempting one. He became the first president to appoint every political seat in the country and made sure he was informed of political situations throughout the country thanks to a new secret police agency. Finally, by early 1940, he decided to strip the autonomy of the universities and place them under government control and supervision. Unbeknown to him, picking on the institutions of higher learning would ultimately bring his downfall.

Although the general had used incredible amounts of violence in 1932, he wanted the people to know that government was there to help. The use of force diminished after 1932. The Hernandez administration would rely on presidential decrees and executive orders when running the country. Whenever a decision or an issue needed to be addressed by congress, the general's Pro-Patria party was always counted on to support their leader.

Besides the central bank, the government created Banco Hipotecario in 1934. The mission of the new private bank was to help give out loans to all landowners in need of one. The bank would become one of the biggest players in the mortgage industry by the end of the Hernandez' administration. The new bank would finally address the need for a credit institution that had been lacking ever since the late 19th century.

The governments creation of a social welfare program came via a new department called Mejoramieneto Social. The new department funded local initiatives and pet projects that would help the working poor. Most of the projects were not very successful in combating poverty or ignorance. In reality, the department was another vehicle for which Hernandez could spread his propaganda.

Finally, Hernandez even challenged the coffee industry elite when he created a state owned coffee company in Compania Salvadorena de Café. The new company was created to loosen up competition and allowed all coffee growers to sell their coffee at competitive prices. Even though the company would lose money as an independent agency, it forced the private sector to open up its doors to other coffee growers. Eventually, both the private and public sectors merged to create a national coffee growers association.

Transition Away From Silver

The lack of silver coins and concerns over counterfeiting led the government to once again issue a decree demonizing all national silver coins on December 23, 1941. The law took effect the following February and the Central Bank was authorized to exchange silver coins for paper money and other non silver coins in circulation.

Unbeknown to the government, the Second War World would create a shortage in general raw materials. Unlike in the previous World War, though, this time the government could not have any mint manufactured coins in non precious metals. In fact, the government placed an order with the United States mint for copper-nickel coins, but was told that due to the war effort, these raw materials were unavailable.

The government had a problem on its hand and had a few options. They could:

a. Release the silver coins that the Central Bank had acquire via the numerous

   decrees and exchange plans.

b. Order new silver or gold coins to circulate

c. Import foreign currency

The government decided that the cheapest and most effective way of dealing with a coin shortage was to have both a combination of new silver coins minted and to import American coins. The government therefore, ordered the importation of 1,200,000 American quarters from the United States mint. Furthermore, the bank authorized the minting of a new 25 cent Salvadorian coin between 1943 and 1944.

The new silver coins are the size of an American 50 cent coin. A million coins were imported for each year all bearing the bust of Federation President Morazán.

Students Fight Back

No matter how many social programs or agencies were created, the general could not stamp out dissent. The biggest obstacle to Hernandez came in the early years of 1940 from an unlikely source; college students. The general underestimated the impact students would make when he chose to take away the autonomy of the universities. The general assumed that the students would fall in line with the rest of the population. However, the general had miscalculated the impact the student's strikes would have on his administration.

It was clear that General Hernandez had become the most authoritarian leader in the history of the state. Although he modernized the country by finally addressing the lack of credit for small farmers and by instituting a social system, he did it by force. The country had clearly become a police state under General Hernandez. Squashing political opposition became the norm of the day and colleges became a prime target for censoring by 1940.

The general failed to see the rich diversity of the student body that opposed his rule. Students came from some of the richest and most prestigious families and others came from a small, but growing middle class of merchants. The college students whom opposed the General would not engage in mob violence, but via peaceful strikes. By taking on the general, the students forced the armed forces to take a stand. Either the army would support General Hernandez or they would support the college students.

General Hernandez in early 1940's decided to change the constitution and to give himself the right to be reelected for a third term. In order to keep order and squash opposition he quickly banned all non government owned newspapers from circulating after their editorial policy questioned the legality of a third term.

Naturally, the general expanded his national guard and police units to areas were political opponents were being aided by sympathetic citizens. He even went so far as to set up road blocks in certain towns, after 6pm, so that no one could leave a town without the consent of an officer. The talk of a third term was enough for the students to call on a national strike of all businesses. This time the students would expand their pacifist strike to include anyone in the country who was willing to stand up to the dictator until he either office or was overthrown.

The general still went ahead with his policy and on January 23, 1944 the legislation controlled only by Pro Patria amended the constitution to extend the presidential term.

Overnight, General Hernandez was given another five year presidential term. The move though became the last straw in the country as many people in all parts of society gathered to join the national strike against Hernandez.

The protest gathered more popularity after the announcement of a third term was confirmed. Many small businesses refused to open or conduct business in areas where students were protesting. As the months passed, more professional ranging from lawyers to government administrators started to either strike or not show up to work. The Hernandez administration was now facing a huge political problem and the use of force, ironically, didn't seem like the logical response.

Although the armed forces showed solidarity, the talk of violence ending the strike unnerved many commanders. Unlike 1932, the people striking were neither poor farmers nor Indians; they were some of the country's brightest young leaders from the middle and upper classes of society. Thus, no one in the Hernandez cabinet felt comfortable using violence to end the national strike. However, talks and rumors of future use of force concerned some army commanders. Those commanders decided to stage a coup in April of 1944.

The coup failed to gather enough military support to permanently remove Hernandez. Instead, the general became more paranoid and started to distrust his own army who was closely linked to many elite bankers and property owners supporting the national strike. The general concluded that only the National Guard and police forces could be trusted to maintain order in the country.

Although Hernandez knew the popularity of the strike cross all socio-economic classes, he decided to play up his populist agenda and claimed that the elite were trying to stop him from creating a state that helped the less fortunate ones. The political ploy failed to gather much traction and by April 24, the students had managed a national strike that was slowly grinding the economy to a halt.

The general and his cabinet didn't respond with force instead they decided to wait it out, hoping that people would quit protesting and go back to their jobs. The strategy turned out to be a disaster, because every day more prominent supporters started joining the cause and soon both the army and the cabinet concluded that they had to let Hernandez go.

The ideological split of the armed forces and the decision not to interfere in the strikes along with the resignation of prominent cabinet members left Hernandez with few allies. Most importantly time was running out. Finally, the death of a prominent Salvadorian-American student, Jose Wright, by security forces was the last nail in the coffin.

The strikers had found themselves a martyr. Soon, the United States ambassador, who many believed was sympathetic to the strikers, visited the general and demanded an investigation into the dead of Wright and a halt to the use of force.

The death of Wright brought together the armed forces and leaders of the strike to discuss a provincial president. Both sides agreed to have General Andres Menendez serve as the provincial president until elections could be held. The general was informed of the decision of no confidence by the armed forces and was told to resign. On the night of May 8 1944, General Hernandez went on the radio to announce his resignation effective immediately.

Although the general was out, the strikes continue. The strikers feared Hernandez would lead a coup to retain power if he stayed in the country and demanded that he go into exile. The army finally agreed to exile Hernandez to Guatemala. On the morning of May 10, 1944 General Hernandez cross the border and left the country.

The Army Strikes Again

The strikers went home and the hope of free presidential elections spread. However, the armed forces had gotten used to holding power and weren't going to be left on the sidelines. It came to a surprise when on October 1944 the most conservative members of the armed forces led by Cor. Osmin Aguire y Salinas staged a coup on provincial president General Andes Menendez. Thus, all but ending any hope for a return to a democratic state. Coronel Salinas was himself a provincial president placed there by the coffee interests in order to choose a worthy successor to Hernandez. On March 1 1945 the elite and the army agreed to place General Salvador Castaneda Castro as president of the country. He would rule for three years.

The coffee interest sector felt that they had re-taken power and although it wasn't a civilian president it was a military officer who was sympathetic to their interests. However, hopes for a return to the good old days would soon evaporate. The armed forces were still a political institution filled with mostly young progressive officers. By 1948 the majority of the army felt that the country needed new leadership and that meant that the elite were no longer going to call the shots.

American Coins Post WW 2

The continuing war effort and the reconstruction of Europe and Asia made acquiring new coins difficult and once again the government had a shortage on their hands. The government once again decided that the best way to deal with this problem was to import American coins in order to circulate as legal tender. However, the government decided to import another 2,500,000 colones or $1,000,000 in United States dimes. The purpose of the dimes was to have them circulate as 25 colon pieces until new ones could be manufactured. The American currency in El Salvador would continue to circulate well into the 1960's when new national currency was available to replace it.

CHAPTER 8 THE YOUTH IN CHARGE: THE BEGINNING OF THE JUNTAS AND MILITARY PRESIDENTS

The fall of General Salvador Castaneda Castro

The hope of returning to a democratic government was sadly short lived after the fall of General Hernandez. Although the new president in General Castro had an administration that was less repressive, it still was a dictatorship nonetheless. By 1948 Castro was seeking to stay in power through legislative elections, however on December 14 1948, he was overthrown by a group of young army officers in what became known as the "golpe de los mayores" or coup of the majors.

Although there had been a history of coups led by generals overthrowing other generals or civilian presidents, there had never been a coup led by lower ranking officers. The coup of 1948 would change the tradition. Several concepts would change in the new regime, that would rule for 12 years, that would establish a precedent for the future juntas. They are the following:

A. The overthrow of the old military rank. From now on, any military officer could lead a junta regardless of rank as long as a majority of his officers agreed to take action. This was the theory, however most junta leaders were at least Lt .Colonels.

B. The establishment of civilian-military juntas. In order to rule with the "consent of the people", the new junta would always seek two or three civilians to share power with. Thus, instead of holding free elections, the military junta would appoint just two or three civilians to share power with.

C. The end of democracy and the beginning of democratic-like governments. The new junta promised to have elections. However, it would continue with the military policy of only having one official party and that party would always win elections. Thus, the government would rig elections and have their candidate win, usually that party candidate was an officer in the armed forces.

D. Government interference. From now on the government would go one step ahead of government interference that began with General Martinez's policies and would force reforms whether or not the elite wanted them. However, real life changing reforms like land reform was something no junta ever successfully implemented.

The idea that the armed forces protected the constitution became the standard doctrine taught to all enlisted men. Because of the unique position of the junta, that included three army officers and two civilians, the majority of the country expected major reforms to take place and a return to democracy in the short term. The Catholic Church and leftist political parties were for the most part behind the new junta led by Col. Oscar Osorio.

As history shows, though, the armed forces had a history of failing to relinquish control of the executive branch for fear of a communist takeover. The new junta not only feared communist, but also the old elite . Coronel Osorio was convinced that either communists or oligarchs wanted to bring down the revolutionary junta for fear of reforms that went against either groups' political ideologies.

The new junta felt that most citizens were hard working and patriotic, but saw that without reforms many would turn to radical ideas and strengthen the far left stand in the country. However, the junta lost support when it became apparent to everybody that it had just become a modern day military bureaucracy out to permanently stay in power through the juntas new political party PRUD.

The new junta passed a new constitution in 1950 that allowed it to intervene and confiscate private property. This finally ended a liberal political system that the elite had enjoyed for over a century. This along with a formation of a new political party, PRUD, that advocated for the ruling party in elections made free democratic elections impossible. In effect, Col. Osorio became the president and won re-election through rigged elections under the guise of free elections.

Col Osorio would bring back the state of emergency thus in effect criminalizing political opposition. He also started to spread propaganda claiming that the state of emergency was necessary because intelligence had reported a threat from the extreme left and right wing forces that wanted to overthrow the junta.

Thanks to the passage of the 1950 constitution, the state could interfere in confiscating private property and in regulating the economy. The state now started to tax businesses that were untouchable years earlier. The state's coffers increased and both Col Osorio and his handpicked successor Col Lemus enjoyed a period of growth in both state and private sector industries.

By 1956, Col. Osorio had decided to support his successor in junta member Col Jose Maria Lemus as president. As was tradition in military regimes, the state organized supposedly free elections, yet the state party's candidate always won, thus Lemus was elected in 1956.

Unlike Col Osorio, Lemus did not have the charisma or the support of his party and allies. The elections that saw him win the presidency was rigged. Furthermore, opposition to this candidacy was surprisingly strong by the combined left and right wing parties. However, worse than being unpopular, Col. Orosio would inherit a major problem that had consistently plagued all Salvadorian governments; the sudden drop of coffee prices.

The junta led by Col Osorio saw that by 1958 the price of coffee in the international market was dropping every year and thus reducing the state's revenue. In order to counter and create a new source of income the state pushed for the implementation of industrial factories and other related businesses in order to generate revenue and jobs. The second stage of Osorio's policy was to create a free trade market among all Central American states. For this policy, he spent a great amount of time in Washington and visiting sister Central American states to draft a policy that would allow Salvadorian goods to enter countries with little or no tariffs. The alliance was never completely strengthened because neither Costa Rica nor Nicaragua wanted to join the alliance. Generally, in my opinion, this would be the last serious attempt at creating a new Central American republic or political union.

The economy under the Revolutionary Junta

The ability of the state to intervene by seizing private assets and taxing coffee was a major political shift from earlier administrations. However, by 1958 coffee began its slow decline that would last for several years and cost the government over 187,500 colones for every $1 loss in coffee by 1958 alone. The failure of the Osorio and Lemus administrations to push for diverse investments in the industrial sector came back to haunt them, since as much as they wanted to distance themselves from the coffee elite in the end, it would be those interests that would push out the revolutionary junta.

Although coffee was still the engine of the economy, the political stability at the time did allow for the growth of the industrial sector to grow for a few years during the 1950's. Between 1951 and 1961 the country saw 10,299 new industrial shops open up creating opportunities for entrepreneurs. However, the majority of the big industrial operations were in the hands of foreigners or the coffee elite whom had diversified their investments. The biggest sectors to open were those related to textile and food manufacturing.

The biggest obstacle to the creation of businesses was the lack of capital. No matter what programs the government instituted, the major banks were still in the control of the small elite families. During the 1940's and 50's various institutions were created to help give out loans to small and middle class businesses. One of the biggest institutions of the Revolutionary Junta was the Instituto Salvadoreño De Fomento a la Producción (INSAFOP) whose main mission was to give credit to those entrepreneurs that couldn't get credit through other bank. However, pressure in the legislative branch soon made it possible for large companies and elite family businesses to obtain loans at more competitive rates from INSAFOP. This also happened with the state-owned Banco Hipotecario which was established in the 1930's to fund small farmers, but by the 1950's was in the hands of the elite who sat on the board of directors and whom changed the rules and policies for loans.

Although the revolutionary government created a new credit agency in Federacion de Cajas de Credito (FCC) to continue funding small businesses at its height, the bank held only $43 million colones. However, the major banks held over $300 million colones. Thus, the FCC would never compete with the big banks.

Although the nation saw more banking institutions founded during this era eventually most would either be consolidated into large banks or would come under the control of the conservatives who quickly made these banks exclusive.

For all the talk of amending the constitution and taking the power to the people, the Revolutionary junta failed to make much of a dent in improving the lives of the majority of its citizens. Worse, the junta never could make coffee and the agricultural sector influence decreased in the economy. The junta found out the hard way in 1958 when the price of coffee gradually started dropping over the course of several years.

This led to less revenue for the government and more unemployment.

All the social improvements and regulations the junta created were somewhat beneficial, but none went so far as to loosen its dependence on a crop that was controlled by only a few wealthy individuals. The revolutionary junta failed to understand that no matter what the political scene was, it would always be dependent on those players that controlled the coffee industry. In the end those elite would do away with President Lemus.

The Revolutionary junta would be overthrown in 1960. President Lemus policies and the failure of the administration to find a true alternative to coffee revenue ultimately sealed his fate. Ironically, it was former President Osorio, along with both civilians and military officials, that decided to end his successor's administration.

The Eventual Return to State Party Politics

After President Osorio was overthrown, a new junta took over and agreed to honor the 1950 constitution. The new junta had a diverse sector of the military and all wanting to see real reform. However, this junta was too dangerous for the old military order. The new junta of government was in power for only a couple of months from October 26, 1960 to January 25, 1961. The conservative members of the army launched a successful coup and installed a Civic Military Directory that would rule for only one year. The old military order was tired of the junta's politics and wanted to return to a one party one, president system. After 1962, the presidents that would hold power would come from the-military sponsor political parties.

The State Control Central Bank

The biggest impact of the short lived junta of 1961 was the major reforms it passed on the central bank. The new junta, decided that the central bank would become a government entity, so that it could better promote equality and expand credit. The objectives of the junta's decisions over the central bank were laid out when it stated its objectives as the following:

a. To promote and maintain monetary conditions
b. Promote the issuance of more credit in order to expand the economy
c. Maintain a healthy and stable currency
d. Coordinate the political economic policies of the country via the central bank

Having the central bank become a part of the government would now make the central bank a political tool for future military presidents.

The first military President

After the end of the civic military directory, the state placed a provisional president in Eusebio Rodolfo Cordon Cea to rule for a year until elections could take place. As was the norm, only military sponsor parties could compete and left leaning parties were banned. The election saw Julio Adalberto Rivera Carballo elected as president. Carballo, a former lieutenant and member of the civic military directory of 1961 ran the country until his term expired in 1967.

However, during Carballo's reign, the armed forces grew more powerful and less tolerant of the left. Eventually, the left-leaning political groups had to go underground and organized to try to enter the political arena again. The army, sensing that it could not control its military sponsor candidates, decided to create an intelligence agency (ANSESAL) and a paramilitary organization (ORDEN) to deal with influential dissidents.

Although the Carballo government tried to invest in infrastructure it ultimately didn't make much of a dent in the country's poor economic climate. The only major policy that the armed forces felt could eventually improve economic conditions was the free trade agreement with allied Central American states that had been the brainchild of President Lemus. However, Carballo's successor would end this agreement with a surprising war on a Central American ally.

The Soccer War

Tensions between Honduras and El Salvador over a border land dispute had been an underlining fault in the relationship of the two countries for decades, yet few experts felt that a war would take place between neighbors in the late 60's. Although Central America had a long tradition of fighting pointless wars in the 19th century, by the 1920's, the states when in dispute, would settle their claims through mediation. The United States was more than happy to mediate disagreements and sometimes would force the states to mediate, since it threatened the Panama Canal zone and American interests in the region.

However, the international community failed to see several political disputes that caused great rifts especially in the case of El Salvador which led to the decision to invade Honduras. Yes, a soccer qualification game for the World Cup did indeed ignite the war, but the root cause was never over a soccer match. The biggest problem between neighbors occurred when in 1968 the Honduran government decided to evict all Salvadorian immigrants from its territory. This decision by Honduran officials was due to the fear that Salvadorian immigrants were invading their country and taking their land. Worse, the Honduran government decided to implement land reform with the seized lands of Salvadorians. Those lands would eventually be re-distributed to Honduran citizens. The military governments of both countries share similar political ideas and problems; however the Salvadorian government had always had the benefit of exiling or exporting their overpopulation to Honduras. By the late 1960's with an already oppressed, but rising left and with American pressure to commit to reforms, the worse nightmare was being realized in the eyes of the military government; the reintroduction of thousands of Salvadorian citizens returning to the country.

The war lasted four days from July 14, 1969 to July 18, 1969 and provided a great victory for the Salvadorian army. However, nothing but international hostility and condemnation was gained by the actions of General Fidel Sanchez Hernandez's regime. In fact the war didn't settle many of the disputes the Salvadorian government had, such as rights for immigrates or border boundaries. The quick condemnation from the United States forced Gen Hernandez to sign a peace treaty with no clear benefits for his side. Although, El Salvador had clearly dominated the war it would not gain any territory.

Repercussions of the Soccer War

If we take into account that the war lasted only four days and that the Salvadorian high command had to conclude its war without any real benefits we would expect that the repercussions wouldn't be severe. In reality, the soccer war would destroy any hope of unification of a Central American union for decades to come and shut down the country out of new markets thanks to a pointless war. In fact, the war cost over $20 million or one fifth of the annual budget. Furthermore just the loss of trading with Honduras cost the state $23 million dollars not to mention the loss of trading with other Central American states. The biggest legacy of the war was the major cracks the military regime exposed that led to a renewed call for a democratic regime and the rise of the left center leaning political parties and ultimately the guerillas.

Coins in the 60's

By the late 1960's, the nation was now fully developing its monetary policy and had enough coins and paper money to fund her needs. The need for foreign currencies was no longer a necessity. Even though dollars still flowed in the market they were no longer considered a necessity for day- to-day operations. Slowly, all the dollars were replaced with colones.

The United States would continue as the nation's primary client and minted all the coins in the 1960's. The decade didn't produce any new coins and the coins that were minted for circulation were those that were in greater need. However, the next decades would add new coins to the daily circulation.

The 1970's

The election of 1972 became the biggest election in decades and many predicted the unified opposition candidates led by Christian Democrat candidate Jose Napoleon Duarte under the banner of the National Opposition Union (UNO) would win. However, like previous military governments, the conservative leadership of the army was against any return to a civilian-military junta, or worse, a return to democracy. The army's candidate in Col Arturo Molina would win a close election, but with many independent observers and the UNO opposition claiming foul play by the military government.

However, not all army officials agreed with the military high command and the younger officers of the army led by Col Benjamin Mejia led a coup to overthrow Molina. Duarte and the other opposition leaders reluctantly supported Mejia, but unfortunately the coup wasn't successful.. Molina retook the government with his loyal troops and decided to exile: Col Mejia, Duarte and all other opposition leaders. This was due to the international pressure not to jail them. However, it was clear that the army was as divided as was the country.

The coup by Mejia weakened Molina's powerbase. President Molina decided to focus on getting rid of all opposition to his rule. He decided that colleges were full of opposition opponents and that taking away the universities' autonomy was the only way of controlling his enemies. His administration exiled or expelled foreign professors and student leaders and placed the universities under military control.

Colonel Molina, seeing that reform was needed and under international pressure, decided to implement agrarian reform by 1976 to calm the opposition and to show the poor that the government did indeed care about land reform. Although the reforms were neither vast nor radical, they were severely opposed by some of the extreme right wing elites and the military high command. His program was opposed on the grounds that it set a dangerous precedent for land reform. His own base didn't support him to the point that his own secretary of defense General Romero threatened to lead a coup if he didn't stop the agrarian reform. Needless to say, Molina suspended any reforms and instead became a lame duck president awaiting for his successor to take over by 1977.

General Romero, the same defense minister who threatened his former boss over any agrarian reform, became the new president in 1977. He exiled his political rival in Coronel Claramount and made clear that he would represent the most conservative wing of both the elites and the armed forces.

"is not the end, it is only the beginning"

Claramount's last words before being exiled would haunt Romero who would become the last military president in the country's history. His extreme policies of repression and intolerance just added fuel to the fire and worried several army officers. After the passage of some extreme laws, such as the law for the defense and guarantee of public order allowing for more detainees and repression, several officers decided to plan a coup. Unlike 1972, the army high command relented and agreed with the younger officers to support a coup led by two brothers Lt Colonel Rene Guerra y Guerra and his brother Rodrigo Guerra.

"cuando no hay balazos el golpe es malo" When there are no bullets, the Coup is wrong

On October 15, President Romeo was informed that the military high command no longer wanted him in power. He quickly resigned and went into exile in Guatemala. Although there was no bloodshed, the extreme right wing forces of the army led by Colonel Gutierrez convinced the high command to throw out the Guerra brothers and to have him lead the new civilian-military junta. In essence, although a new government with civilians was now in power, the armed forces still ran the country. Unfortunately, once again, due to selfish special interest, the armed forces decided to scrap any reforms. By the end of 1979 the country was politically split and talk had turned to violence. By the end of the year the country was engulfed in a civil war.

CHAPTER 9 INTO THE ABYSS: THE CIVIL WAR 1979-1992

The Civil War 1979-1992

The civil war was the longest and most tragic war the country had ever experienced. I will provide only a brief summary of the civil war and the implications it had in the production of coins.

I think Dr. Stephen Webre summarizes the army's vision of democracy as one that "encourages an active opposition, but by definition, forbade the opposition to come to power." This explains the entire political system in El Salvador for the past 80 years.

The new civilian-military junta would be called the Revolutionary Government Junta (RGJ) and took power in October 15, 1979. Once again, the army was calling for their kind of reform. Needless to say, that the banned political parties were outraged that the new junta would not call for elections. However, instead of returning to the underground, elements of the far left decided that armed combat was the only way to overthrow the army.

Unto An Uncertain Period

The 1970's would become the tipping point in the class struggle between the few elites and the working class people that would ultimately trigger the civil war. The economic policies of the military regimes never addressed desperately needed economic reforms.

Thus, the lack of attention by the army led to many young people joining underground political parties. Some of these parties sought peaceful change while others believed in the use of force to obtain power. Within a few years, many moderate and left wing politicians started to openly challenge the military governments. The stolen election of 1974 by the army was the last straw and many people decided that the only way to change the government was to abandon politics and prepare for a war.

Coins of the 70's

The central bank's policies had shifted very little ever since the 1960's reform junta. However, the bank was still under government influence. The new decade brought the largest amount of coins produced ever since the early 20th century. The decade would see the re-introduction of commemorative silver and gold coins. Although, none of these coins were minted in El Salvador, they all celebrated important anniversaries during the 1970's.

The re-introduction of the commemorative coins was a boom to collectors. The last issue of commemorative coins occurred in 1925. The central bank would re-introduce the commemorative set by producing the most diverse set of gold and silver coins to commemorate the 150th anniversary of independence.

Four designs were minted for each gold coin. Gold coins were minted in the following denomination : 25,50,100 and 200. Each coin had a different design to illustrate an important aspect of the nation. The silver coins were minted in one and five colon denominations. The one colon has the distinction of carrying a design from Spanish artist Salvador Dali. Needless to say, the Central bank went out of its way to design a historic collection of coins.

However, the central bank was not done in minting commemorative coins. The 1977 Central American bank conference gave the central bank another opportunity to mint silver and gold coins. Both of these coins were minted by the British Royal Mint.

These coins have an interesting design. The bust of the coin resembles a coin from the old Central American Federation with a sunrise near one of five volcanoes representing the original five republics of the old federation. The reverse of the coin features a prominent detail seal of the republic.

By the end of the 1970's, the political instability had not stopped the central bank from ordering and planning new coins. However, the central bank would once again become the target of influence by the various military juntas who felt the need to influence the bank's policies in order to retain and expand power. The civil war would finally end the banks" independence" and make it a branch government.

1980's The Civil War

The junta proposed new solutions that they were convinced would immediately result in reform. The same old problems and solutions were placed on the table. The reforms included: land reform, higher wages, political freedom, etc.

However, the junta decided that it needed to control the central bank in order to accomplish the goals it had set forward. Thus, on October 15, 1979 the junta took over all the shares of the central bank citing the lack of credit equality to the working class and too much influence by the elite families. The new central bank would now become a branch of the federal government. This at least helped the bank from losing more money.

A report issued by the Inter-American Development Bank (IDB) reported that the economy was being destroyed by capital in-flight and lack of investment by

1979. By 1980 the bank reported that in the preceding years the country had lost over $1 billion through the exporting of colones on the black market. The banks were losing around $800,000 every day and by mid 1981 only four banks were solvent, not including the central bank. Private capital had fallen from a high off $159 million in 1978 to an outflow of $176 million in 1979. In essence, the country was on the road to a depression.

The junta finally nationalized the central bank by 1982; however the damage had been done. Without the millions of dollars and tons of food provided by the United States to fight the war; the country would collapse. It's estimated that Washington poured in over $200 million a day to strengthen the government at its height.

The one Colon coin returns

Under these political conditions, the central bank would continue to re-order new coins throughout the 1980's. The idea to bring back the colon coin was finally realized in 1984 when the central bank reintroduced a new colon coin, the first in over 70 years. However, the idea that the new colon coin would be welcome was quickly abandoned when popular opinion turned against the use of the coin. The coin's large size and weight made it unpopular among people who preferred to use paper money over the coin, much like our experience with the Sacajawea coins; the colon would never replace the paper bill.

The War

Scholars point to 1979 as the year of the coup that led to the open of hostilities. However, the assassination of the country's highest Catholic Church leader in Monsignor Oscar Romero, an outspoken critic of the army, by the extreme right wing intelligence on March 24, 1980 led to a full blown war breaking out days later.

The beginning of the war was chaotic as both sides tried to reign and attract opposition political members. The junta's policies alienated some of the country's most conservative supporters. Its civilian junta members that represented the moderate political sphere also weren't content. The first civilian-military junta failed to accomplish the goals it had listed. As a result, the civilian junta members resigned and the first junta fell.

However, Colonel Gutierrez quickly assembled a second civilian-military junta. Under this cloud of instability, the civil war would consume a great number of the nation's resources and lives for the next decade. Thus, the junta was forced to extend its hand in order to gain civilian members, even those civilians the army didn't care for. Much of the pressure to bring in a variety of political parties to share power came from the United States government who was concerned over the image the army was giving the world.

It's ironic that the main opposition party in the Christian Democrats led by Napoleon Duarte (returning from exile) would fill the void in the junta's civilian leadership role. Duarte, once the army's top enemy, became the army's spokesperson. However, tensions on both the army's side and the Christian Democrats' would ultimately lead to the fall of the Second Junta. However, pressure from Washington to hold elections would force the army to retreat from politics and have elections.

The army, for its, part failed to unify its forces against an inferior cash strapped guerilla movement throughout the course of the war. In fact, the army seemed to have had a mix agenda. Instead of combating the guerillas, many troops attacked civilians killing thousands of innocent bystanders. Its intelligence divisions and police units became infamous for killing: top opposition political leaders, college students, priests and anyone who dared offer an opinion not favorable of the army. In essence, government forces were split three ways: fighting the guerillas, fighting civilians, and the last one eliminating intellectuals and freedom fighters. Is it any wonder, that with all the money and military support from Washington that the war ended in a stalemate?

The guerillas, or as they were known, the FMLN fought a long successful war of attrition. Although they forced a stalemate and peace, many have argued that the guerillas could have held on longer for better terms. The vast opposition included, several political factions, such as: communist, liberal Christians, and several businessmen. Although none of these supporters had much in common, all had been disappointed with the numerous military juntas and felt armed combat was the only way to force political change.

Just like government forces, some guerillas committed atrocities. As a result of some bad people in the movement, the guerillas lost support. Although by the end of the war it had done a better job of improving its image and keeping order. As a result, the guerilla movement easily became a unified political party after the war.

All civil wars are tragic and destructive. The civil war lasted 12 years and over 75,000 civilians were killed in the process. No one can argue that this war could have been avoided. Tension had been building for decades against military interference of the political system. The various military juntas and presidents couldn't solve the country's vast social economic problems. The Soccer War, brought thousands of expatriates back to a country that couldn't offer them any hope. With an overpopulated country and a large segment of the population living in poverty, it was only a matter of time before a war would break out. As a result of the army's reluctance to either land reform or an economic plan, the country fell apart. In the end, the nation would eventually get what was lost in all the ideological rhetoric of the war and that was: a true democracy.

CHAPTER 10 A NEW BEGINNING AND THE END OF THE COLON: PEACE AND GLOBILIZATION IN THE 21ST CENTURY

The Beginning of Reconstruction

The civil war would come to a conclusion in 1992. The central bank was already figuring out a plan to rebuild the country. During the war, two presidents Napoleon Duarte of the Christian Democrats and Alfredo Christiani of the ARENA party slowly chipped away at the army's influence in politics by being elected presidents in free elections. It was their policies that once again gave the central bank their autonomy.

The civil war ended with the peace accords signed in Mexico City on January 16, 1992. From that day on, the country had to rebuild with the help of not only the UN, but also with private capital. The peace accords laid out several agencies and departments that would help speed the re-construction period, including the integration of the FMLN into the political forum.

Like all recently ended civil wars, both sides were reluctant to embrace each other. As a result, although the country was slowly being reconstructed a sharp political ideology divide had grown to open hostility between the two dominant political parties in the ARENA and the FMLN. Sadly, this political intolerance is still evident today.

In the economic sector of the economy, the state quickly encouraged banking institutions to loan and to improve conditions for investments in the country. By the mid- 1990's there were several Salvadorian banks that were competitive in the Latin American banking community. As a result, by the late 1990's, the banking community felt that it was time to introduce a radical reform to the state's economic engine that they felt was needed to attract even more capital into the country. The idea of dollarization suddenly became a policy many conservatives and bankers thought could push El Salvador into becoming one of the most sought after countries for investments. Soon after, the ARENA party made it is mission to pass legislation to not only formally dollarize the nation, but to fade out the colon from the economy.

Coins minted in the 1990's

The central bank ordered two commemorative coins one in silver and one in gold to commemorate the end of the civil war and another to commemorate the 500th anniversary of the discovery of America. These coins would be the last commemorative issues the state would order in the 20th century.

The remaining issues were a variety of coins in circulation that continued with the large orders and diversity of denomination as in the past decade. With the exception of the 50 cent piece, the state would continue to order coins for the remaining denominations throughout the 1990's. Unlike in past decades, the minting of coins would take place through a variety of private and government mints throughout the world after the US mint stopped minting world coins in the late 1980's.

Free Market Reforms

The various right wing governments that ruled El Salvador in the 1990's began privatizing many government holdings and opening up commerce to the world. The result was an economy that depended less on agriculture and more on the service industry and the remittances send home by millions of immigrants, mostly from the United States.

The new market opportunities were a boom for the few with credit at their disposal, but sadly once again, a large number of the population didn't benefit from the opening of the markets. The fact that many citizens lives improved had more to do with remittances than with opportunities the government created through the privatization of many industries. The large number of refugees that fled the civil war ended up in various parts of the world and decided not to return, but to send back their money in order to improve the lives of their loves ones.

Regardless, of the outcome of economic reforms after the civil war, the economy had improved. Therefore, the idea to replace the colon with the dollar started to take hold in the late 1990's.

The Dollarization and the end of the Colon

The end

The idea of dollarization is a very complex theory that takes several years to be proposed and framed to the general public. Plus, it takes several political compromises for it to be presented in a legislative branch for a vote. After which the central bank needs to educate the masses and prepare for the withdrawal of its local currency for the dollar. It generally takes several years for a financial policy of dollarization to take effect.

However, in the case of El Salvador, the entire process took 39 days from the time it was propose to when it was approved by congress. Yes. It took the government only a month and a week to completely overhaul the entire monetary policy of the country.

On January 1, 2001 the monetary integration law took effect. The law made several important monetary policies:

    a. Would fix the colon to 8.75 to the dollar
    b. Made the dollar legal tender in the country
    c. Allowed Euros, Pounds and Yens to be traded
    d. Peg the colon to the dollar

Of all of these laws, the most important one was the dollarization of the colon. In essence, it marked the end of the colon. It took several months, but eventually the colon started to disappear with the dollar replacing it. Today, although, colones are still legal tender, they are scarcely used.

It seems ironic that the government decided to rush the policy of dollarization without a history of financial crisis. Unlike, Argentina or Mexico, the Salvadorian central bank had done a pretty good job at keeping inflation down and maintaining a competitive currency in Latin America. Ever since 1994 the colon had been pegged to the dollar at a reasonable 8.75 colones per dollar. Why than dollarize?

The government had decided that it needed to become more competitive and that dollarization was the only way it could keep interest rates low and attract foreign investors. Unfortunately, the ARENA party representing the right wing establishment, didn't take into account all the problems the country would face if it no longer controlled its financial destiny.

The decision to dollarize seemed like a good idea, however the government failed to take into account that dollarizing is just one requirement in making the country competitive to foreign investors. The government unfortunately, has done little in terms of expanding education for the masses and in expanding credit to its citizens. There is a major segment of the population that still relies on pawn shops and loan sharks for loans, thus many people can't enjoy the benefits of having lower interest rates due to dollarization.

However, the biggest problem the country has had for the past several years is the high level of crime involving gangs. No foreigner wants to invest in a country where they or their employees risk harm when you have a competitive safe country like Costa Rica nearby. Sadly, the many conservative administrations have failed to deal with public safety.

Having the United States dictate monetary policy seemed like a good idea back in 2000 prior to 9/11 and the housing crisis. However, ever since then, the country has been linked to America's monetary policy and high debt and it's at the mercy of the United States central bank and its policies. I hope that remittances sent back to the country won't dramatically drop or that investments don't falter otherwise the country will have to seriously cut in its infrastructure, thus reducing foreign investment.

Finally, the fact that it only took 39 days from the date President Flores announced his intention of dollarizing to passing the monetary law in congress is shocking, since many didn't take into account the loss of a national symbol in the colon. Granted, not many

Salvadorians are collectors, but many are proud of their heritage and the loss of the colon was the most recognizable symbol. It took El Salvador over 50 years after her independence to establish a mint and several decades to maintain an accurate monetary supply in the country, yet the decision to do away with the monetary coin was done without any concern to its heritage.

The colon survived decades of military dictatorships and incompetent administrations to become a stable currency. The monetary policy of the country by 2000 was better than those of major countries in Latin America. The country never defaulted on her debt. Yet, the colon was done away with without much input from the people. Unfortunately, the Flores administrations ignored the will of the people for it was more convenient to adopt a policy than to debate it in public.

The colon leaves a rich numismatic legacy to its people and to the world. Many of its early coins and bills are prized by collectors for their beauty and rarity. Unlike many countries that chose to display its leaders, El Salvador chose to display its heroes on her coins. Heroes like: Morazán, Delgado, Arce… and even Columbus.

The legacy of the colon will no doubt increase as future generations will rediscover a part of their heritage and hopefully spread it among future generations. As for collectors, the opportunity to own Salvadorian coins will no doubt increase over time, since it is highly unlikely that the country will ever return to the colon system. Regardless of why people collect colon coins one thing is sure, El Salvador leaves behind a rich and proud numismatic history.

Chapter 11: Collecting History

Why Write about Salvadorian Coins?

I am amazed as to how much information the numismatic community has collected and the spirit of goodwill that many experts have decided to share their knowledge with collectors. It is a rarity to find a topic regarding an American coin that has not been thoroughly written about by a numismatist. Sadly, I would learn that the numismatic community in other countries didn't share the same passion or knowledge we Americans take for granted.

The topic of Salvadorian coins didn't really come up as often with my family. Yes. I had many recent issues of colones added to my collection, but I was never really interested in studying the history of those coins. I wrongly thought that the colon coins had been studied and written about by many numismatic experts. Though, as I have gotten older and with recent political events in the old country, I decided to learn more about El Salvador.

The recent spike in gold prices in the last couple of years got my attention and I remembered stories my parents had told me about large gold coins that had circulated in El Salvador, but they gave no specifics. Curiously, I checked the most recent Krause World Coin Catalog to find that no such coins were to be found. In fact, Krause had only the most recent and popular coins listed in the catalog.

Thus, I was determined to check the city's library achieves for past Krause catalogs. I found these coins in previous publications of the world coin catalog. There were several coins listed, including the silver and gold coins minted. Unfortunately, the only gold coins minted were in small quantities in the late 19th century, therefore whatever coins my parents mentioned could not have been Salvadorian. The mystery surrounding the origin of these coins and others led me to start focusing on the nation's past. In the process, I learned more about El Salvador than I ever intended too.

The hardest part about researching this topic was that there is truly a lack of information regarding most coins that were minted and circulated in the country. Once I learned that the country didn't mint coins until after 50 years of independence, I could see where the lack of money led to a huge disparity between the notorious ruling families and the majority of working citizens. I am convinced that the lack of a national currency in the mid-1800's, along with privatizing and confiscation of Indian lands, led to the huge income disparities that would become the source of the majority of the violence that would plague the state in the 20th century.

Why, no currency? Why no central bank? Why no financial package reform during economic crises? I had a hard time getting answers to my questions. Most of the recent history books that dealt with El Salvador focused on the political struggle and military dominance in politics that led to the bloody civil war.

However, very few books exist that covered the financial history of the nation. The few numismatic books found on Salvadorian coins are not only rare, but also written in Spanish. Even those Spanish books couldn't be found through the library or through a numismatic organization A few of these books had to be imported through a specialty bookstore. In essence, finding any books regarding any part of the numismatic history of El Salvador, whether they be coins or bills, is difficult.

Finding books and sources on coins in El Salvador is difficult due in part to the lack of government documentation that existed in the last century. There are two reasons why documentation for 19th century coins is missing and probably lost to time. One is the lack of revenue the government had in the late 19th century that forced many presidents to lay off many government employees and to incredibly stop documentation. Secondly, what little paperwork was recorded was achieved in the government's hall of records which was destroyed in a great fire in 1899. Thus, many questions about the 19th century records on coins have been lost to history.

When we talk about 20th century records we face a different problem. Unlike in the previous century, government revenue was sufficient, is just that no one bothered to leave detailed documents regarding coin orders in the early 20th century before the central bank took over minting orders. Add to this problem, the government allowed the private banks in the country to order coins for the state and didn't bother to keep detailed records of these transactions. Whether government bureaucracy or corruption is why there is today many missing data on currency is also a matter of debate. What is true is that after the establishment of the central bank currency and coin documentation improved greatly.

It really is a mystery as to what coins could have circulated or were counter-stamped during the early 19th century. Although, we have records of counter stamp coins that have been certified as authentic, there are many stories and even coins that have been claimed to have been re-stamped or to have circulated in the country. Could Chinese money have circulated in the 19th century? Could $5 American gold pieces have circulated as the main gold coin of choice? Unfortunately, I feel, we will never know the answers to these questions. However, I hope that our fascination with collecting will help some future collector address these questions and add to the numismatic library of Salvadorian coins.

Collecting

Like most developed countries, there are few coins that were issued in short supply and we now lack enough information on these rare coins. The scarcity of these coins has elevated their value as more people, thanks to technology and coin grading companies, have decided to collect them. The room for counterfeit coins still exists today, but even the most novice collector is aware of the basic grading services available to them. The internet has made auction sites much more accessible to collectors selling their coins worldwide. Thus, the opportunity to collect complete sets of world coins has never been easier for the collector.

Having said that, the fact that the colon no longer circulates in the country has made it more difficult for collectors to build their sets. The way I have built my collection has been through the use of various auction sites. I think eBay is the best place to purchase coins. eBay has a wide variety of Salvadorian coins for auction. Most silver and copper coins can be found on any given day. However, gold and counter stamp coins are a rarity. I caution collectors interested in buying rare Salvadorian coins that are not certified by either: NGC, PCGS or ANA.

Major coin auction sites like Heritage and Stacks focus on the rare coins. I have found numerous gold and counter-stamped Salvadorian coins that cannot be found anywhere else. Most of the coins sold through these auctions are already graded and certified. Buying could become expensive since the buyer has to usually pay a 15% premium on every winning item to the auction house.

However, it's worth it since you will find many rare and one of a kind coins you won't find anywhere else in the world.

Like all countries, you will always find several coins that were issued for circulation that have become scarce throughout the years. In the case of El Salvador, there are a few coins that are rare for the collector to acquire in the open market. Most of the 19th century coins prior to independence are rare for collectors to acquire, especially those that were made by the state as provincial coins during the brief existence of the Central American Federation. Once every few years, you will see a provincial coin up for auction at either: Heritage, Stacks or a third coin auction site. These coins are extremely rare in any condition.

Below is a list of the most popular and rarest coins to collect. However, I don't address either provincial or counter stamp coins, because many are extremely rare and expensive. And in the case of counter stamp coins many are one of a kind. The following coins are sometimes hard to acquire, but can still be found with some due diligence in the market. These are the most sought after coins.

Gerardo Barrios Coins

The popular liberal president of the 1860's was the first chief executives to order Salvadorian coins for the state. The lack of documentation for this series has made them extremely rare. Many fakes are in circulation. A large number of Barrios counterfeits were produced back in the late 1960's. These coins were minted in all precious metals except platinum.

These coins are for the most part, rarely graded by either the NGC or the PCGS. This only adds to the uncertainty in verifying them. Most of the coins minted were made out of copper. The majority of coins minted were made at the Turin mint. The Krause world catalog lists several variations of the Barrios coins. As to the origin of any real Barrios gold coins, it is a mystery. However if they were minted, they were most likely pattern coins meaning only a handful of pieces were ever minted. Accordingly, there has never been a gold Barrios coin graded by any third party grading company. There are a few silver coins in circulation that have been graded, however these coins rarely ever go on the auction block.

Sample: Gerardo Barrios 25 centavo coin

The Original 1892 coin set

Frankly, the most important set to acquire is the 1892 set. Even though it is difficult to find a complete set, it's not impossible to build one from scratch. Although this pursuit would set collectors several thousand dollars back, their scarcity will prove to be a good investment over time.

Breaking down the 1892 set into denominations:

The Flag coins

There are two flag coin designs that were minted. They are the 50 and one peso coins, both have the same design. These silver coins circulated for a few months, but were recalled when the government decided to have Columbus appear on the colon coins.

Most of these coins were recalled and melted, however a few hundred did survive.

Acquiring either coin is not difficult. Many of these coins show up every few months on eBay. However, expect to pay upwards of $50 dollars for an ungraded 50 cent piece. The one peso coin usually shows up at auction and a collector can expect to pay over $400 for an ungraded specimen.

I notice that several of these coins are not graded when auction on eBay. This could be due to a lack of interest by collectors. However, these coins can easily be counterfeited. Having said that, though, a collector can get a good price buying an ungraded flag coin.

1 Centavo Cap Coin

The only coin minted by the CAM that was not approved by the Salvadorian government was the one centavo coin. The coin was minted from copper and was not previously discussed between the Central American Mint LTD and the government. As a result, the majority of one centavo coins were melted down and only a few thousand specimens remain.

The coin is rare and unlike other coins from this series, more prone to counterfeiters due to its simple design and material. I have seen several counterfeit copies on eBay from sellers who claimed that these coins are authentic. There is even a website company that manufacturers "replica" coins. On its website, a picture of the one centavo coin appears. Apparently, this coin has been determined to be both rare and easy enough to counterfeit. I urge extreme caution when buying this coin if it's not encapsulated and graded.

Although this coin is rare it is not expensive or hard to find. A collector can expect to pay more than $200 for a graded sample.

The Gold Series

The most prestigious coins minted by the state of El Salvador for circulation were the four gold coins minted in 1892. These coins are not only rare, but beautiful in design making them very valuable to the collector. The four coins minted were the: 2 ½, 5, 10 and 20 peso gold coins. Unlike, the majority of coins for circulation this set were only minted in 1892 and there were only a few coins minted for each denomination.

The 2 ½ gold has 500 coins, the 5 peso has 400 coins, 10 peso coin has 300 and the 20 peso coin has only 200 coins minted.

None of these coins are found on eBay; however they do appear every couple of months on prestigious coin auction houses. Expect to pay a few thousand dollars for each coin whether they are graded or not.

Samples: *the four gold 1892 colones*

The Colon Series 1892-1896

The collection of colon coins minted in silver are some of the best coins minted for the state of El Salvador. The collection is not difficult to acquire and a collector can expect to spend a few hundred dollars to acquire a complete set. The 50 cent piece coins are also affordable and widely available. These coins are common enough to find on eBay every few weeks, with the exception of the 1896 date.

In my experience, I have never run into this coin in any auction. It's amazing that this coin is rarer than a 2 ½ gold peso coin. In fact, analyses of both the census and population report by NGC and PCGS show that only a few coins have ever been submitted for grading. Those few coins that have been graded are of poor quality.

Sample, 1892 one and 50 centavos Columbus colon

The 5, 10, and 20 centavo coins

The rest of the set of coins can be found for a few dollars on the internet and completing a set is also very easy to do. These coins are very simplistic in design, but they were made out of silver.

Sample: the 5, 10 and 20 centavos coins

The 1909 ¼ Real Coin

The most mysterious coin in the history of El Salvador has to be the ¼ real coins. As we had discussed earlier, there are so many questions about the origin of this coin that folklore has surrounded it for decades. The rarity and scarcity in the open market for this coin adds to the value. The coin can set a collector back a few hundred dollars and I strongly suggest that a collector acquire this coin after being graded by one of the legitimate coin grading companies due its ease of counterfeiting.

Sample: ¼ real coin of 1909

Commemorative Coins

1925 San Salvador Anniversary

In celebration of the 400th year founding of San Salvador the state ordered a set of commemorative coins to be given out to foreign dignitaries. The state placed an order with the Mexican mint to mint a total of 2,000 silver one colon coins and 200 gold 20 colon coins.

These coins have become the most popular and valuable commemorative coins for Salvadorian collectors. The silver coin is widely available on eBay and other auction sites. Expect to pay around $225 or more for an ungraded specimen.

The gold coins minted are a lot more difficult to acquire and much more expensive due to its scarcity and high gold content. A few of these coins can be acquired every few years at auction houses like Heritage or Stacks. Even though there were 200 of these coins minted only a handful actually are sold or traded every few years. Expect to pay upwards of over $4,000 for a graded coin.

Sample: 1925 1 colon coin

Sample: 1925 20 colones coin

1971 150th Anniversary Set

The most diversify set of coins minted for the state of El Salvador has to been the silver and gold series of 1971. Each coin minted displayed a different design on every denomination. The set includes the famous Salvador Dali sculpture "La Fecundidad" on the silver one colon and gold 25 colon coins.

-
-

The Silver coins

The silver set has two coins with the denomination of one and five colones. The one colon has the famous Dali sculpture "La Fecundidad" and the slogan "Lucha por la dignindad del hombre" (fighting for the dignity of man). The five colon coin has a winged liberty statue and a small bust of Guatemalan priest Jose Simeon Canas y Villacorta. The reverse of both coins have the national seal. The silver one colon has 2.93 grams of silver and is .999 pure. The five colon coin is 11.50 grams and also .999 pure silver.

Sample: 1971 1 and 5 colones

The Gold coins

There were four gold coins minted each with a different design and denomination. All coins are .900 pure gold. The 25 gold colon piece has the same Dali design the silver one coin has. It has 2.95 grams of gold. The 50 colon coin has the same design as the silver five colon coin. It has 5.90 grams of gold. The 100 colon coin has the map of the Americas with El Salvador being magnified for all to see. This coin has 11.80 grams of gold. While the 200 colon coin has the Panchimalco church. This coin has 23.60 grams of gold. The reverse of all coins have the national seal and the bust of Guatemalan priest Villacorta.

Although these coins are not rare, they are rarely sold as a set. Expect to pay over $1500 for a complete set. However, individual coins can be acquire on EBay for a few hundred dollars. An average price for the gold: 25 colon is $115, 50 colon $300, 100 colon $525 and 200 colon $850. The silver one colon can be acquired through eBay as low as $10 and the five colon for $20.

Sample: 25, 50, 100 and 200 gold colon set

1977 18th Annual Governors Assembly

The 18th annual Central American bankers union was held in the country. To celebrate the meeting ,the central bank ordered from the British mint a set of coins to commemorate the event. The interesting design on the bust resembles a replica of an old coin of the Central American Federation with the sun rising from one of the volcanoes representing Central America. This is the only set where more gold coins were minted over silver ones. A total of 2,000 silver coins were minted and a total of 4,000 gold coins produced. However, when it comes to proof coins 20,000 were minted for silver and only 400 for the gold series. The silver denomination is 25 while the gold is 250 colones.

These coins are not rare. The silver variation whether coin or proof coin can be acquired through eBay for around $30. The gold coin is a little rarer, but expect to pay around $ 700 for one not graded.

Sample: 1977 Gold 250 colones & 25 silver

1992 Discovery of America and Union For Peace

    The last set of commemorative coins minted celebrated the 400 years of the discovery of America and the Peace Accords that ended the civil war. Both sets of coins were minted in both silver and gold. The Independent coin features a map of the world and the three Spanish ships Columbus sailed with to America. The Peace Accord coin features on its bust a set of four clasped hands commemorating peace. Both silver coins were minted at a face value of 100 colones while the gold coins had a face value of 2500 colones.

Although these coins were the last commemorative issues, they are not easily found in the market. However, recent developments in the spike of both gold and silver have brought out many of these coins to market. Both the silver and gold coins weighed almost one ounce. The collector should expect to pay almost the value of that coin's precious metal content, plus a small premium for the numismatic value of the coin.

Sample: 1992 Peace and Discover gold and silver coins

Not Released for Circulation

There were two coins that were planned for circulation that were never released. However a few of these coins made it out into the hands of collectors. The 1997 five colon coin and the 2000 five colon coins were planned and manufactured in small numbers. The 1997 five colon coin has the exact design as the commemorative 1992 discovery of America coin. The coin is unique, because it is not only bi-metallic, but has a Braille edge for the blind to recognize it! This coin was reportedly minted in 2000, but for some reason carries a 1997 date.

Sample: 1997 5 colones coin set

The 2000 five colon coin is also bi-metallic. However, this coin is unique since it actually commemorates the Y2K scare. Apparently, the central bank was just as shocked as to the speed of dollarization, since it was planning new colon coins. Therefore, none of these coins were mass produced. Both of these coins are very rare and the few that do show up in the market will command top dollar, possibly a few hundred dollars.

Sample: 2000 5 colones coin

CHAPTER 12: 20TH CENTURY COINS BY DECADE

Introduction

A variety of new coins hit the market after the closure of the CAM in the 20th century. Most of these coins were either minted in the: United States, Great Britain, Belgium and the private mint, the Birmingham. The United States, though, minted the majority of the coins for several decades.

However, in the late 1980's the US mint would stop minting coins for foreign governments. This decision forced the Salvadorian central bank to choose from a variety of new mints to produce new coins. As a result, the central bank authorized other mints such as the Canadian mint and the German mint to produce coins in the 1990's.

All the regular coins minted for the next 100 years would have the bust of only three leaders on them. They would be: Federation President Francisco Morazán, Christopher Columbus, and father Jose Matias Delgado. The overwhelming majority of coins would have a portrait of Morazán. The explanation as to why is simple. The Salvadorian government had been the most loyal supporter of the old Federation and President Morazán. Many former Salvadorian presidents had always advocated for a new union between the Central American states after the collapse of the federation.

In the minds of the many politicians of the era, a possible alliance of the Central American people was possible either through a unified country or through free trade agreements. Furthermore, the country would see many autocratic and military presidents dominate the presidency for the next couple of decades. It was determined that it was better to have a man whom every Salvadorian would agree was the example of what a president should be than in having a controversial leader on her coins. Thus, President Morazán would show up on most coins throughout the 20th century.

I have listed the coins minted by decade in the following pages. Each section has a brief description of the coins minted in the decade, with the exception of the commemorative coins (see collecting history for commemorative coin info).

1900's

The coins produced during the first decade of the new century were a continuation in both design and denomination as the old CAM peso coins produced between 1892 and 1896. The country's legislation decided to allow the banks to mint one peso coins starting in 1904. Once a shortage of coins was produced in the mid 1900's the administration decided to have two new peso coins minted with the years of 1908 and 1909 on each one peso coin.

There were a few modifications to the peso coin. The coin's bust of Columbus is a little wider in the shoulder region and all coins had the new dates of production stamp on them. The coins were minted in the United States, but none have an American mint mark. Besides the one colon coins minted, the only other coin minted during this decade was the unique ¼ real coin.

The One Colon Coins

The ¼ Real coin

The ¼ real coins production is surrounded in mystery. As a result, many myths have emerged to explain its existence. First, we have no idea where this coin was minted. Rumors have persisted for decades that this coin was minted in El Salvador, possibly as a pattern coin. However, although the coin is rare, large quantities in circulation (around 50,000 pieces were minted) therefore it is not a pattern coin.

There are a few records that discuss why this coin was minted. A question often asked is whether the country wanted to return to the real system. Perhaps, but the only realistic answer was that it needed a small denomination coin to circulate to satisfy demand. It seems that the lack of small denominations during the 19th century continued plaguing the country well into the first half of the 20th century.

We know that the coin was minted in 1910, yet has a 1909 date. We also know that a legislative proposal to increase small denominations in rural areas was the proposal that led to the ¼ real being minted.

Finally, we know that the coin was so unpopular and many merchants were rejecting it that the legislative branch decided on July 10, 1911 to recall all ¼ real coins from circulation. The only mystery that has yet to be resolved is where this coin was minted and the possibility that the state actually experimented with minting coins again after the closure of the CAM.

¼ real (value at the time 3 1/8 cents), copper, no known mint, 50,000 minted

1910's

The decade brought new coins for circulation. For the first time in decades, new designs were circulated with new denominations that would make day to day market transaction more convenient.

The first sets of coins issued for circulation in this decade bear the 1911 date and include the: one colon, 25 centavo, 10 centavo, five centavo and one centavo coins.

The one centavo coins

The first one centavo coins minted show the date 1913 and are similar to the 1889 one centavo coin minted by the Birmingham mint. The one centavo coins were made of copper-nickel and would be in circulation from 1913 to 1936.

The bust of the coin features President Morazán surrounded by the words Republica Del Salvador and the date in the bottom center. The back of the coin has the words "1 centavo" surrounded by a wreath.

The 3 centavo coins

The state commissioned the manufacture of new three centavo coins in 1913 that were similar to those minted in 1889. The new coins were minted by the Birmingham mint in copper nickel in two installments one featuring the 1913 date and the other one with the 1915 date. The coin's bust featured President Morazán surrounded by the words Republica Del Salvador and the date in the bottom center. The back has the "3" centavo denomination and words surrounded by a wreath.

The 5 Centavo Coins

The design of the five centavo coin would change twice in less than four years after being minted and would display new designs, since the original five cent pieces minted by the Central American Mint LTD. The first five centavo coin minted was at the Birmingham mint out of silver and feature an exact design much similar to the 1892 piece. These designs were active between 1911 and 1914.

The 1915 five centavo coin would change course and for the first time include the bust of Central American Federation President General Francisco Morazán. The bust of President Morazán would become a feature in many of the nation's future currency, since he was probably the most known Central American leader of the past century. The back of the five centavo coin featured the number "5" surrounded by a wreath and centavos in the center of the coin. These coins were minted throughout the United States mints and were manufactured between 1915 and 1925. All of these coins were made out of copper-nickel.

The 10 centavo coins

The 10 centavo coin was minted in silver by the Birmingham mint between 1911 and 1914. The coins designs were similar to those of the Central American Mint Ltd minted In 1892 that feature the national emblem in the bust and the "diez centavos" surrounded in a wreath in the back.

The 25 centavo coins

The 25 centavo coin was minted by the Birmingham mint and the 1911 coin is similar in design to the one minted by the CAM in 1892. The bust of the coin has the national emblem in front with the words "Republica Del Salvador" and the .835 content of silver and year 1911 numbers on the bottom of the coin. The back of the coin features the "veinte y cinco centavos" wording surrounded by a wreath.

The 1914 design would differ in the national emblem and wording of the coin. The new design that appeared on the 1914 edition is similar to that of the 1914 five centavo coin. The bust of the coin features the new national emblem surrounded by a wreath and the words "Republica De El Salvador En La America Central". The 1914 date and a small star appeared next to the words. The back features the words "veinte y cinco centavos" surrounded by a wreath.

The 1 Colon coins

The new one colon coins minted bear the 1911 date and would have the same design of Columbus as the 1892-1896 coins and the 1904-1908 designs. The coins would be minted from silver and they would all be minted in the United States and in Belgium.

The 1914 Belgium series is reported to have been melted due to a small order. There are a variety of American colon coins in the market. However, there is a rare proof series of about 20 pieces minted in the United States. One proof coin was sold in 2007 for $15,000 at auction.

The 1920's

The new decade brought new hopes that the economy of the country would continue expanding internationally, however both struggles at home and financial collapses by the end of the 1920's would bring an end to the nation's democratic tradition.

The new currency minted for El Salvador would continue to emphasize lower denomination, for example, the colon coin was no longer minted. By the new decade the government had stopped minting silver coins and all the coins minted during this decade would be made of a copper nickel.

The design of the few coins did not change from the previous decade and only three denominations were minted, those coins were the: one, five and 10 centavo coins.

The 1 Centavo Coin

The design for the one centavo is exactly the same as the previous set minted in the 1910's. The new one centavo coins minted are from the following dates: 1920, 1925, 1926, 1928.

The 5 Centavo Coin

The design of the five centavo coins minted in the 1920's are exactly the same from the 1915 Morazán set that was used to mint the remaining 5 centavo coins for the rest of the decade.

The 10 Centavo Coin

The design of the 10 centavo coin remains the same compared to the previous decade. The coins were minted of copper nickel. There were only two date's minted 1921 and 1925.

The 1930's

The 1930's would be the slowest numismatic decade in the 20th century due to many political and economic problems the country experienced. The young democratic process was ended when vice president General Maximiliano Hernandez Martinez led a coup that overthrew President Araujo. General Martinez would establish the longest personal military dictatorship of the century in the country.

During the dictatorship of General Martinez, the country saw a restructuring of the political landscape. The 1932 Massacre along with a global economic depression led to a consolidation of power all directly controlled by General Martinez. The decade saw no coin orders being processed or minted during the 30's with the exception of the one centavo coin. The 1930's would be the slowest decade in the history of the 20th century in terms of coin production.

The most important event during the dictatorship of General Maximilano Martinez was the founding of the central bank in 1934. The central bank finally gave the bank the sole authority to print and mint coins on behalf of the state and thus no longer had to rely on private banks for such orders.

The dictatorship of Maximilano Martinez lasted 14 years from 1930 to 1944 and would leave a sad tragic legacy that would be the foundation of future absolute dictatorships and injustice for decades to come.

The 1 Centavo Coin

The only coin minted during this time or that has a 1930's date on it is the 1936 one centavo coin. The coin is made up of copper nickel and was produced in the United States.

The 1940's

The 1940's brought a new decade with new challenges that would force the government to seek alternative production of coins and bring back the use of silver coins all due to the massive war effort during the first half of the 1940's. During this decade four denominations were minted, they were the: one, five, 10 and 25 centavo coins.

The 1 Centavo Coin

The one centavo coins minted in the 1940's would have two different metals. The initial 1940 production was of copper nickel material. Soon after the production of this set, the nation requested another set of copper nickel coins. However, World War 2 had just erupted and raw materials were being set aside for military use. Thus, the future production of the one centavo coins were to be made of the available material: bronze.

The 5 Centavo Coin

The use of different metals to produce coins would become a common theme during the decade and the five centavo coin would have two different metals use for the set. In fact the 1944 set would feature two different coins with two different metals, one copper nickel and the other one copper nickel zinc.

The 10 Centavo Coin.

The only 10 centavo coin minted was manufactured in the United States and has the year 1940. The coin is composed of copper-nickel.

The 25 Centavo Coin

The most interesting set of the decade has to be the large silver 25 centavo coins minted with the 1943 and 1944 year. As was mentioned earlier, the use of silver had been slowly made obsolete by the state, but the lack of raw metals forced the government to reconsider its policy. The coins were needed in the country and the government had no other choice, but to order silver coins from the United States.

The coins are fairly large and heavy. The coins were minted with a design similar to those of the five centavo coins of the decade with President Morazán in the bust and the 25 centavos surrounded by a wreath in the reverse. The 25 centavo coin is one of the most sought after and collectible Salvadorian coins of the era. The detailed design of Morazán on the bust and the fact that the coin was made out of silver in an age when silver was being discontinue, has made this coin a collectible. The coin is a very affordable coin in the set, setting the collector a few dollars back to acquire.

The 1950's

The new decade brought more stable governments, sadly though, military governments. The 1950's was a time of prosperity in the United States, but a time of rebuilding in El Salvador.

As far as the coins produced during the decade, we would continue to see a need for small denominations in circulation, thus a focus on small coins continued while the expansion of paper money took care of large denominations. The new decade would see the last silver coins minted for circulation, those being the 1953 25 and 50 centavo coins. Thus, after 1953 El Salvador would no longer use silver in any coins minted for circulation. The only usage of the precious metal would come in the form of commemorative coins.

There were four denominations minted during this period, they were the: one centavo, 10 centavo, 25 centavo, and 50 centavo coins.

The 1 Centavo Coin

The one centavo coins continue to circulate with the exact same design of President Morazán on the bust and the one centavo surrounded by a wreath on the reverse. The coins were all minted in the United States and were made of bronze.

The 10 Centavo Coin

The 10 centavo coins produced show two dates 1951 and 1952 and were made of copper-nickel. The design of the coins is traditional compared to the previous 10 centavo coins minted since 1921 showing the bust of President Morazán and 10 centavos surrounded by a wreath on the reverse of the coin.

The 25 Centavo Coin

The 25 centavo coin and the 50 centavo coin are the only coins this decade that would display a new design. As it was traditional and cost effective, the bust of President Morazán graces the majority of coins regardless of denomination during the past couple of decades.

The new 25 centavo coins would show for the first time a patriot of the Salvadorian independence in the bust of father Jose Matias Delgado. Unlike, President Morazán who is known for being the President of the Central American Federation, father Delgado is known in El Salvador as the leading figure of independence for the country. The addition of father Delgado bust to the new 25 centavo coin opened the door for his continuing usage in future denominations. Along with the 25 centavo coin, the 50 centavo coin was also minted in 1953 with father Delgado.

To add further importance to this new coin, this 25 centavo piece would be the last silver coin issue for circulation in the country's history. The coin was minted in the United States.

The 50 Centavo Coin

The minting of a new denomination would further help the citizens in their day to day activities. The addition of the 50 centavo piece was a throwback to the late 19th century the last time any 50 centavo pieces were minted for circulation. It had taken almost five decades for the new 50 centavo piece to be re-introduced to the public. The new 50 centavo coin was also made of silver and features the bust of father Jose Matias Delgado. Both the 25 and 50 centavo coins were minted in the United States and outside of their size and denomination; there is no difference in design between either coins.

The 1960's

The new decade brought more of the same political and social problems to the forefront in the country. During this period the gap between poor and rich was starting to show and new political parties and movements started to finally take off. The coins produced during this time continued to stress small denominations over large ones and the usage of non-precious metals now became the standard policy of the government.

The 1 Centavo Coin

The one centavo coin produced during this decade was a continuation of the same design use in the previous decades with President Morazán's bust on the cover and the one centavo surrounded by a wreath on the back design. All coins were produced of bronze and they were all minted in the United States.

The 5 Centavo Coin

The five centavo coins minted also didn't change in terms of design, with the bust of the coin showing President Morazán and the reverse showing five centavo surrounded by a wreath. All coins were of copper-nickel and were minted in the United States.

The 10 Centavo Coin

The 10 centavo coins minted were a continuation of previous designs with the bust of President Morazán on the cover and the reverse showing 10 centavo surrounded by a wreath. All coins were of copper-nickel and were minted in the United States.

The 1970's

The 1970's proved to be the most politically active and chaotic decade so far. It saw the rise of new political groups and new brutal policies by the military governments that sought ways to squash popular resistance. By the end of the decade, the various governments remained unstable and it was clear to many that the new decade would ultimately bring more bloodshed.

The coins produced during the 1970's offered for the first time in decades, a variety of new denominations to enter the market for circulation. There were a total of six different denominations, including for the first time, the minting of a new 50 centavo coin that was not made out of silver and the three centavo coin.

The 1 Centavo Coin

The new one centavo coins for the first time would have two different sets issue with two different metals. The 1972 issue was a continuation of minting bronze one centavo coins from previous decades. It also would mark the last time the government would order any one centavo coin in bronze.

The next set of 1976 and 1977 would keep the same design as all previous one centavo coins minted in the 20th century, but would be made up of brass. The coin's bust shows President Morazán while the reverse shows one centavo surrounded by a wreath. The coins were minted in the United States.

The 3 Centavo Coin

The new three centavo denomination was originally minted for the first time in 1913 and by 1915 the coin was no longer minted and thus became a short lived denomination. However, the government decided that by 1970, the country was in need of small denominations and was willing to have new three centavo coins minted and tested in the marketplace. The new coins featured the bust of President Morazán and on the reverse the three centavo surrounded by a wreath. The coin was made out of nickel brass and was minted in the United States. The 1974 coin is the only three centavo denomination coin minted in the 1970's.

The coin was not popular and a further study by the government led to its withdrawal in future minting orders. Never again would we see the three centavo coin in production. The coin's odd denomination and withdrawal by the government however has not made this coin a collectible piece.

The 5 Centavo Coin

The five centavo coins produced during this period would also be made up of two different metals. The 1972 and 1974 set were made up of copper nickel while the 1975, 1976 and 1977 sets were made out of copper clad steel. The bust of the coin features President Morazán and five centavo coins surrounded by a wreath on the back. All coins were minted in the United States.

The 10 Centavo Coin

The 10 centavo coins minted during this decade would use two different metals for the three different years. The 1972 set was made out of copper-nickel and continued the country's recent history of copper-nickel production of 10 centavo pieces. The 1975 and 1977 coins however would be composed of different metals.

The 1975 10 centavo coin was made out nickel clad steel while the 1977 coin set was made out of copper nickel.

The bust of the coin features President Morazán while the reverse features the 10 centavo surrounded by a wreath. The coins were minted in the United States.

The 25 Centavo Coin

The new 25 centavo coin minted, would for the first time, not be minted out of silver. In this set, the coins would be produced out of nickel. The bust of father Jose Matias Delgado, would once again, grace the bust of the 25 centavo piece; the continuous use of father Delgado on 25 centavo pieces would become the norm.

The bust of father Delgado graces the front of the coin while the reverse shows 25 centavo surrounded by a wreath. The coins were minted in the United States.

The 50 Centavo Coin

The new 50 centavo coin minted would also be the first set to be minted since 1953 and the first set minted that wasn't made out of silver. The bust of father Delgado graces the front of the coin while the reverse shows 50 centavos surrounded by a wreath. The coins were minted in the United States.

The 1980's

The 1980's would be the decade that devastated the country once the civil war erupted in late 1979. The various short-lived military juntas that overthrew each other did nothing but escalate the tension between the military and the civilian population. Various groups were created by both the military and the population to force their political views on the general public. However, the brutality to which a great number of right wing groups terrorized the civilian population, ultimately led to an armed conflict pitting the military government and her allies against the various leftist groups that would unite to form the FMLN. The civil war would be devastating and would last almost 12 years from 1979 to 1992.

Under this intense climate, many new coins were nevertheless issued for circulation, including the return of the colon coin in 1984. As unstable as the country was, the central bank continued its operations even though by the 1980s the bank was basically bankrupt.

New Octagon Design for Coins

A new design for the 1980's was introduced that would change the appearance of future coins minted. Although the basic features of the coins would be kept, they would be surrounded by an octagon shape around the bust of the feature.

The 1 Centavo Coin

The war did disturb production of coins due to either financial problems or protest by countries that didn't want to do business with the government. Thus, the one centavo coin for various reasons, have a number of coins minted with various metals. The first coin, the 1981 set is made out of copper zinc and is the only coin minted with a date in the early 1980's. The explanation for a lack of coins being minted around this time could be that the initial start of the war experienced the heaviest fighting and thus kept most government agencies, including the central bank at bay. However, new one centavo coins were minted for 1986 that were made out of copper clad steel. The 1988 issue was made out of brass plated steel and the 1989 one centavo coin was made out of brass clad steel.

The designs of the one centavo didn't change with the bust of President Morazán and the date on the cover and the reverse showing one centavo surrounded by a wreath. All one centavo coins were minted in the United States.

~ 236 ~

The 5 Centavo Coin

The new editions of five centavo coins were minted out of copper clad steel and stainless steel. The design of the coin didn't change the other previous five centavo coin for the 1984 issue and 1986 set. However, the size of the coin by 1987 did change and the coins size would be smaller. The bust of President Morazán is now surrounded by an octagon around the coin, but the reverse design is the same as previous editions.

The 10 Centavo Coin

As with the previous five centavo design, the new 10 centavo coins would be smaller then previous editions and the bust of President Morazán would be encircled by an octagon. The new design would become the standard design for future 10 centavo coins. Only two dates were minted in the 1980's; the 1985 coin made out of copper zinc nickel and the 1987 coin made out of stainless steel.

The 25 Centavo Coin

The 25 centavo coins with the 1986 date continued the design of the previous set. But just like the previous five and 10 centavo coins; the new coin would have father Delgado's bust encircled by an octagon on the cover by the time the 1988 edition came out. The 1988 edition is larger than its predecessor. Both coins were minted in the United States.

The 1 Colon Coin

The expansion of coins from the late 1940's had included the expansion of denominations such as the: three centavo coin and the 50 centavo pieces. However, the one colon pieces were left out of any future production due to the fact that paper money was satisfying the need for any colon denomination in coins. Unlike, in the early 20th century, by the late 1940's the central bank had done enough to print paper money. By the 1980's the government had decided to re-introduce the one colon denomination much like the three centavo coin in 1974 and await the public's response.

The initial 1984 one colon coin featured the traditional bust of Columbus as was the case with every one colon coin since 1892 (exception, the 1892 silver flag). However, several changes were made to the coin that made it more contemporary compared to its predecessors. For example, even though the Columbus bust is still shown on the face of the coin, the Republica De El Salvador surrounds the bust instead of his name or the one peso denomination. The year is also now front and center on all colon coins, something that was left for the reverse of the coin in previous editions. The reverse of the coin replaces the national emblem and Republica De El Salvador with the one colon denomination surrounded by a wreath. The size of the

coin was smaller and the coin was made out of copper nickel for the first 1984 and 1985 run instead of silver. The 1988 edition would be made up of stainless steel.

The 1984 Colon proved to be a major disappointment to the central bank. The public was not happy with such a large and heavy coin being in circulation and preferred the paper equivalent instead. The government's implementation of the coin was to save money, because producing coins in the long run was cheaper and longer lasting than paper money.

Use of the coin fell and the government felt compelled to issue studies and even issued press releases to confirm the benefits of the coin. No matter what the government said, the public rejected the new colon coin. In fact, the coin acquired the nickname "suegra" (mother -in- law), because no one wanted to be stuck with the coin. The colon coin was re-designed somewhat for future issues, but it would remain in circulation.

The 1990's

The beginning of the 1990's was more of the same in terms of the civil war climate. Neither side had taken advantage of the battles fought or the resources available to them. By 1992, an agreement was made with the help of the United Nations to end the war and rebuild the country with both political ideologies sharing government responsibilities. The agreement finally ended the 12 year old civil war and finally allowed the country to focus on her infrastructure and to start thinking about expanding her economy.

The decade also brought important changes to the numismatic history of the nation. The United States, decided in the late 1980's, to stop minting coins on behalf of other nations. This decision impacted El Salvador, since most of her coins had been produced in United States mints. Therefore, by the 1990's most of the coins minted came from a variety of countries, including: Canada, Great Britain, Germany and others. The variation of countries minting coins allowed for a number of coins to be minted in different metals and designs.

Finally, the most important financial event in the country's history would occur by the start of new millennium. It started as a theory, when several economists started to propose that the economy dollarize in order to take advantage of the country's strong business policies. The proposal became a reality when the legislative branch approved the proposal to adopt the dollar as the monetary unit of the country by the year 2000. The 1990's became the last decade when the colon would be minted and it ended the 100 plus years of the colon. By January 1, 2001 the nation would start to use the United States dollar and coins in their day- to- day activities.

The 1 Centavo Coin

The last one centavo coins minted were made out of brass clad steel and only two years were minted, they were the 1992 and 1995 editions. The design of the coin was traditionally the same as previous coins with the bust of President Morazán on the front and the one centavo surrounded by a wreath on the reverse.

The 5 Centavo Coin

The new coins produced during the 1990's were minted in various countries of various metals. The design of the coin is the same compared to the previous five centavo coins. The bust of the coin features President Morazán while the reverse has the one centavo around the wreath. The coin's metals are: copper clad nickel steel for the 1991 and 1997 edition, nickel clad steel for 1992, 1993, and 1994, 1995 editions, copper clad nickel steel for the 1998 edition and nickel clad steel for the 1998 and 1999 sets.

The 10 Centavo Coins

The 10 centavo coins minted in the 1990's were of similar pattern to those of the 1980's in that the size and design were similar. The bust of President Morazán is again surrounded by an octagon around the coin while the reverse shows the five centavo surrounded by a wreath. Two metals were used for the production of the 5 centavo coins, they were: nickel clad steel and cooper nickel clad steel.

The 25 Centavo Coin

The design of the 25 centavo coin didn't change from the 1980's. The design consisted of the bust of father Delgado on one side and the 25 centavo surrounded by a wreath on the reverse. Several metals were use for the coins, they were: stainless steel, nickel clad steel and cooper nickel clad steel.

The 1 Colon Coin

The last one colon coins minted were of the same design as the late 1980's colon coins with the bust of Columbus surrounded by an octagon around the coin and the reverse showing one colon surrounded by a wreath. The metals uses on the coins were: stainless steel, nickel clad steel and copper nickel clad steel.

Bibliography Books

Almanzar, Alcedo F and Stickney Brian R. The coins and paper money of El Salvador. San Antonio: Almanzar Coins of the World,1973

Almeida, Paul D. Waves of Protest : Popular struggle in El Salvador 1925-2005. Minneapolis: University of Minnesota Press, 2008

Cabrera Arevalo, Jose Luis. Las Controversiales Fichas de Fincas Salvadorenas. San Salvador: Universidad Technologica de El Salvador ,2009

Callejas, Jose. Indice Cronologico. Universidad Francisco Gavidia, San Salvador.2002

Editorial Oceano. Enciclopedia de El Salvador Volume 2. Barcelona,Editorial Oceano, 2001

Guttag, Julius. The Julius Guttag Collection of Latin American Coins. New York, 1929

Hinds, Manuel. Playing Monopoly with the devil. New Haven,CT , Yale University Press 2006

Jovel, Roberto J. La Historia Numismatica de el Salvador Vol 1 San Salvador,1999

Jovel, Roberto J. La Historia Numismatica de el Salvador Vol 2, San Salvador, 2002

Karnes, Thomas L. The Failure of Union. Durham: The University of North Carolina Press, 1961

Krause, Chester and Mishler, Clifford. Spain, Portugal and the New World. Iowa: Krause Publications, 2002

Lindo-Fuentes, Hector. Weak Foundations: The economy of El Salvador in the nineteenth century. Berkeley: University of California Press, 1990.

Llack Ulloa, Roberto. The Tokens of El Salvador Santiago de Maria: San Salvador, 1980

Loveman, Brian and Davies Jr, Thomas M. The Politics of Antipolitics: the Military in Latin America. Wilmington: Scholarly Resources Inc, 1997

Montgomery, Tommie Sue. Revolution in El Salvador: from civil strike to civil peace. Boulder: Westview Press Inc, 1995

Parkman, Patric. Insurrecion no violenta en el salvador: la caída de Maximilano Hernandez Martines San Salvador 2003

Sweeny, James O. A Numismatic History of the Birmingham Mint. London: Birmingham Mint, 1981

Turcios, Roberto. Autoritarismo y modernización: El Salvador 1950-1960. San Salvador, 2003

White M, Christopher. The History of El Salvador. Westport: Greenwood Press,2009

Wilson, Everett Alan. La Crisis de la integracion nacional en El Salvador 1919-1932. San Salvador : Direccion de publicaciones e impresos, consejo nacional para la cultura y el arte, 2004

Government Publications

El Salvador. Diario Official. San Salvador, 1890-1950

United Kingdom. Royal Archives.The Central American Mint LTD. London, 1890, Certificate of Incorporation

Magazines

Hancok, Virgil " Featuring Fakes: Do you have the original?" The Numismatist December 1970 Pg 1776-1777

Hancock, Virgil " Featuring Fakes" The Numismatist. February 1978 Pg 272-273

Kraus, Ernst " New and Recent Issues" The Numismatist June 1976 Pg 1268-1269

Kraus, Ernst "New and Recent Issues" The Numismatist May 1975 Pg 1039

Numismatic Scrapbook "Current Coins" The Numismatic Scrapbook, June 25 1971 Pg 642

Numismatic Scrapbook " Original Dies 'Restrike' El Salvador Pattern, May 25, 1971 Pg 554

Stickney, Brian R "Case of the Missing Mint: Mystery off Salvador ¼ Real, 1909" World Coins February 1974, Pg 350-352

The Numismatist "Metal and paper currencies of the Americas" The Numismatist January 1932 Pg 80

Wallace, Holland " Additional Information El Salvador Mint Report" The Numismatic Scrapbook September 1965 Pg 2697

Western Publishing Co Inc" Current Coins of the World" The Numismatic Scrapbook, May 25, 1973 Pg 450

Web Publications

Bloomberg. "El Salvador's Greenback Bind" *Bloomberg Businessweek*. October 17, 2005 Web. 11/22/2010

Dickerson, Marla " In El Salvador , the dollar is no panacea" *Los Angeles Times* August 4, 2007. Web 7/1/2010

Towers, Marcia and Borzutsky, Silvia "The Socioeconomic Implications of Dollarization in El Salvador" *Latin American Politics and Society* Volume 46, Number 3, Fall 2004 Pg 29-54 . Web 7/10/2010

www.ingramcontent.com/pod-product-compliance
Lightning Source LLC
LaVergne TN
LVHW052100090426
835512LV00036B/2743